Monetary Divergence

Michigan Studies in International Political Economy

SERIES EDITORS: Edward Mansfield and Lisa Martin

Monetary Divergence

Domestic Policy Autonomy
in the Post–Bretton Woods Era

David H. Bearce

The University of Michigan Press   *Ann Arbor*

Published in the United States of America by
The University of Michigan Press
Manufactured in the United States of America
⊚ Printed on acid-free paper

2010   2009   2008   2007   4   3   2   1

A CIP catalog record for this book is available from the British Library.

Library of Congress Cataloging-in-Publication Data

Bearce, David H., 1967–
    Monetary divergence : domestic policy autonomy in the post–Bretton Woods era / David H. Bearce.
        p.   cm. — (Michigan studies in international political economy)
    Includes bibliographical references and index.
    ISBN-13: 978-0-472-09961-0 (cloth : alk. paper)
    ISBN-10: 0-472-09961-2 (cloth : alk. paper)
    ISBN-13: 978-0-472-06961-3 (pbk. : alk. paper)
    ISBN-10: 0-472-06961-6 (pbk. : alk. paper)
    1. Monetary policy—History—20th century.   2. International finance—History—20th century.   3. Macroeconomics—History—20th century.   I. Title.   II. Series.

HG230.3.B43   2007
339.5'3—dc22   2006015258

To Dana,
whose loving support made this book
and everything else possible

Contents

Tables

Figures

Acknowledgments

I would like to thank three different research communities for the valuable contributions that they provided to the research presented in this book. Because the very first version of this research project took the form of my doctoral dissertation at Ohio State University, I begin by offering my thanks to Ed Mansfield, David Rowe, Tim Frye, and Eric Fisher for helping me get started on the project and for then keeping me on track. I also thank a fellow student in the field of international political economy (IPE) at Ohio State, Pat McDonald, who provided lots of useful comments on the many drafts of my chapters and papers related to monetary policy divergence among advanced industrial democracies.

My second round of thanks goes to the research community at the University of Pittsburgh, where I began writing this book as an assistant professor. I am grateful to my colleagues in the Department of Political Science, including David Barker, Chris Bonneau, Chuck Gochman, Michael Goodhart, Mark Hallerberg, Anibal Perez-Linan, Sebastian Saiegh, Dan Thomas, and Tony Walters for substantive and methodological comments or suggestions that found their way into the manuscript. In particular I also thank Nita Rudra, who volunteered to read multiple drafts of the manuscript. Her insightful feedback led me to restructure my arguments in an effort to reach a broader IPE audience.

My third research community is the ever-expanding set of scholars devoted to international and comparative monetary politics. For instructive comments on these topics, as well as for setting professional examples that I have deliberately tried to imitate, I thank Bill Bernhard, Lawrence Broz, Bill Clark, Mark Hallerberg, and Jerry Cohen. I also offer sincere thanks to Jonathan Kirshner and Eric Helleiner, who organized a workshop devoted to the manuscript for this book in November 2005 at Cornell University. I feel honored that so many prominent scholars, including Phil Cerny, Kate McNamara, Layna Mosley, Lou Pauly, Chris Way, and Michael Webb, attended and offered their criticism and suggestions for improving the manuscript. I have not been able to follow all of their advice, but I hope that this book is much improved as a result of trying.

Finally, I offer my genuine thanks to two anonymous reviewers for their helpful and encouraging comments about this book's manuscript and to Jim Reische, who shepherded me through the peer review process for the University of Michigan Press. I am honored to be associated with the series Michigan Studies in International Political Economy, which has published some great books on the topic of monetary politics.

Deborah Patton built the index for this book, and her work was supported by a grant from the Richard D. and Mary Jane Edwards Endowed Publication Fund at the University of Pittsburgh.

CHAPTER I

Introduction

International capital mobility is an undeniable fact for the advanced industrial democracies in the post–Bretton Woods era. Whether capital mobility is measured in terms of fewer government restrictions or in terms of growing financial flows, one can easily observe that it has reemerged as a leading feature of the international monetary system after attempts to restrict capital movements across national borders during the Bretton Woods regime.[1] After a long debate about the causes leading to the return of international capital mobility—focused largely on whether this development was due more to technological advances outside of government control or to deliberate government choices for capital liberalization[2]—political scientists are now focused on understanding its consequences.

The political science discipline has made substantial progress in understanding the political consequences of international capital mobility and economic globalization more broadly. But many important questions remain largely unanswered, especially those related to national monetary politics and policy.

How does international capital mobility constrain the monetary policy choices of national governments: in terms of policy goals (such as inflation), in terms of policy instruments (such as interest rates), or both?

If international capital mobility constrains national monetary policy choices, has it produced systematic monetary policy convergence?

1. For evidence on capital restrictions, see Quinn and Inclan 1997. For evidence on capital flows, see Simmons 1999.
2. On technological advances, see Bryant 1987. On deliberate government choices for capital liberalization, see Helleiner 1994.

Can we observe monetary policy convergence in the exchange rate regimes constructed by the advanced industrial democracies in the post–Bretton Woods era?

If systematic monetary policy convergence has not occurred, what factors help explain the patterns of monetary policy divergence after 1973?

These questions remain largely unanswered because the economic globalization research program tends to focus more on government spending and related fiscal policy choices than on national monetary policy and related exchange rate outcomes. To see how this has been the case, it is useful to group the growing political science literature on the consequences of international capital mobility into three broad waves (see table 1).

Beginning in the early 1990s, the first wave of relevant literature proposed the broad macroeconomic policy convergence hypothesis, including the proposition that international capital mobility constrained both fiscal and monetary policy choices of national governments.[3] While this policy convergence argument was supported by interesting case examples, it effectively eluded systematic empirical testing until the mid-1990s. At this time, the second wave of research began more rigorous testing of the policy convergence hypothesis. But most of the empirical work focused on government spending choices, where political scientists concluded that fiscal policy divergence remains possible in the post–Bretton Woods era,[4] at least for the advanced industrial democracies.[5] Much less empirical work was devoted to national monetary policy and de facto exchange rate stability.

TABLE I. Three Waves of Political Science Literature on Monetary Policy Convergence

First wave Early 1990s	Offered the broad macroeconomic policy convergence hypothesis, including both fiscal and monetary policy convergence
Second wave Mid-1990s	Tested the macroeconomic policy convergence hypothesis, finding evidence of fiscal policy divergence Less research devoted to monetary policy and exchange rate stability
Third wave Late 1990s	Offered new explanations for monetary cooperation and integration, generally accepting the monetary convergence hypothesis

3. For key academic works, see Scharpf 1991; Garrett and Lange 1991; Kurzer 1993; Cerny 1995. For extensions into more popular literature, see Ohmae 1995; Greider 1997; T. Friedman 1999.

4. For key works, see Garrett 1995; Garrett 1998b; Iversen and Cusack 2000; Burgoon 2001.

5. Rudra (2002) shows how this conclusion may not apply to less-developed countries.

This research trajectory has produced an interesting tension in the political science literature concerning the effects of international capital mobility. While most scholars now accept the conclusion of fiscal policy divergence, many also accept the largely untested hypothesis of systematic monetary policy convergence. As Mosley (2000, 739) observed in her review of this literature, scholars have demonstrated "cross-national diversity in such areas as government consumption spending, government transfer payments, public employment, and the level of government tax revenues" yet acknowledge a "growing cross-national similarity in aggregate monetary [policy]." Yet without completely divorcing monetary policy decisions from those of national fiscal policy, how can we sustain a story of systematic monetary policy convergence next to all the evidence of fiscal policy divergence?

Indeed, rather than directly confronting the proposition of systematic monetary policy convergence, a third wave of literature in this research program seems to treat the phenomenon largely as given, debating instead the possible causes of monetary cooperation and integration, especially with regard to events in Western Europe.[6] Thus, political scientists are currently focusing their attention on whether European monetary convergence—and, by extension, that of the other advanced industrial democracies—stems more from the role of transnational neoliberal ideas or from political pressure applied by international exporters and investors who favor monetary integration to achieve exchange rate stability. But trying to explain monetary policy convergence becomes problematic if we cannot establish that the supposed phenomenon is actually occurring. On this point, Clark (2003, 2) argued, "while this 'convergence' view of the current international political economy is widely accepted, there is virtually no evidence to support its main dynamics."

I. Research Puzzles

Although this book explores all the questions posed in the introductory section of this chapter, it is usefully organized around two primary research puzzles. First, can we observe systematic monetary policy convergence among the advanced industrial democracies in the post–Bretton Woods era? The analysis that follows will focus primarily on this cross-sectional and temporal domain, because it is where those who argued for systematic monetary policy conver-

---

6. For two major third-wave contributions, see McNamara 1998; Frieden 2002. I would also put Oatley's 1997 book into the third wave, since that study sought to explain monetary cooperation in Western Europe, although Oatley was careful to acknowledge divergent cases.

gence staked their theoretical and empirical claim. This first research question is harder to answer than it may appear, because the political science literature on international monetary policy has not developed a suitable operational measure for external monetary convergence or for the corresponding loss of domestic monetary autonomy. As I will demonstrate later, the rough measure that our discipline has sometimes employed—membership in a regional monetary regime or other de jure commitments to fix the value of the national currency—is rather poorly suited to the task. Thus, it is hard to make confident inferences about the loss of domestic monetary autonomy and external monetary convergence by looking at institutional commitments alone.

If—after developing more suitable operational measures for these concepts—the answer to the first research question is yes, then we can place the systematic monetary convergence hypothesis on a much more solid empirical footing. This would surely be a valuable scholarly contribution. But if the answer is no—that is, if the advanced industrial democracies have pursued different monetary policies with little evidence in favor of systematic monetary policy convergence—then we need to explore a second and related research question: what factors can explain the patterns of monetary policy divergence among the advanced industrial democracies in the post–Bretton Woods era?

In this book, I use the term *monetary policy divergence* to refer to the situation where the advanced industrial democracies used their national monetary policy to achieve different economic objectives, with some governments working toward external currency stability and other governments using monetary policy for more domestic purposes.[7] This conception of monetary policy divergence borrows heavily from a prominent macroeconomic model known as the Mundell-Fleming framework. This macroeconomic model posits that when capital is internationally mobile—as it has been for the developed countries since at least the early 1970s—governments must choose between exchange rate stability and domestic monetary policy autonomy. If they choose external currency stability, they give up the ability to direct their monetary policy instrument toward certain domestic economic objectives. If governments use their monetary policy for certain internal objectives, then the external goal of exchange rate stability will ordinarily become unachievable given international capital mobility.

Thus, the second research question can be restated using language from the Mundell-Fleming framework. In the post–Bretton Woods era, what factors have led national governments to choose domestic monetary policy autonomy,

7. For an earlier statement on this subject, see Bearce 2002.

accepting greater exchange rate variability with international capital mobility? Similarly, what factors led them to opt instead for exchange rate stability, accepting the loss of domestic monetary autonomy?

2. The Argument in Brief

With regard to the first research question, whether there has been monetary policy convergence among the advanced industrial democracies in the post–Bretton Woods era, I will make the case that there has been much less than the conventional wisdom of systematic monetary policy convergence would expect. To reach this conclusion, I first create operational measures for both domestic monetary policy autonomy and exchange rate stability, using the interest parity condition from open-economy macroeconomics. The interest parity condition suggests that domestic monetary autonomy can be identified by a nominal interest rate differential: the extent to which the domestic interest rate differs from the prevailing external interest rate. A larger interest rate differential indicates greater domestic monetary autonomy, while a smaller differential indicates more external monetary policy convergence.

The empirical evidence reveals that many advanced industrial democracies have maintained relatively large interest rate differentials since 1973, the beginning of the post–Bretton Woods era. Indeed, there has been no strong trend toward smaller interest rate differentials, as would be expected by the systematic monetary convergence hypothesis. To the extent that monetary convergence can be measured indirectly by looking at exchange rate stability, the evidence also shows no pattern of more stable exchange rates for the advanced industrial democracies since 1973. Consequently, the post–Bretton Woods era is better understood as a period of monetary policy divergence, defined as the situation where the advanced industrial democracies use their national monetary policy to achieve different economic objectives, with some governments working for greater external currency stability and other governments using the monetary policy instrument for more domestic purposes.

I will also make the case that this situation of monetary policy divergence is directly related to the well-documented phenomenon of fiscal policy divergence among the advanced industrial democracies after 1973. With this goal in mind, I offer a theory based on the government's fiscal and monetary policy mix to show how a government's spending decisions help explain the national interest rate and related policy outcomes. This policy mix theory posits that when governments choose to spend more to promote economic growth, provide public goods, or engage in income redistribution, they must also raise the domestic interest rate for inflation control. A higher domestic interest rate usually translates into a larger interest rate differential, relative to the nominally low "world" interest rate. A larger interest rate differential, in turn, means greater exchange rate variability in an era of international capital mobility.

The policy mix framework allows us to define a set of economic policy choices consistent with domestic policy autonomy in the post–Bretton Woods era: more government spending, a higher national interest rate, a larger interest rate differential, and greater exchange rate variability. If governments desire external policy convergence, they must move in the opposite direction with regard to fiscal and monetary policy. Less government spending permits a lower national interest rate, which, in turn, facilitates a smaller interest rate differential and reduced exchange rate variability, or greater external currency stability.

Consistent with the theme of policy—including monetary policy—divergence, I will show how different governments belonging to the Organization for Economic Cooperation and Development (OECD) have made policy decisions in both of these directions since 1973: some governments have opted for domestic policy autonomy, while others have worked for greater external policy convergence. Indeed, to the extent that there has been any dominant trend since 1973, it appears to be toward greater domestic policy autonomy; hence, the present book is subtitled *Domestic Policy Autonomy in the Post–Bretton Woods Era*. While there has been some policy convergence on the part of certain national governments, it has not occurred on any widespread basis. Put somewhat differently, episodic choices for external policy convergence cannot be treated as evidence of systematic policy convergence when there are as many, if not more, governments who have made the opposite choice for domestic policy autonomy.

For some political scientists, this may appear to be an unsurprising conclusion. Indeed, it might be argued that monetary policy divergence has been obvious in the post–Bretton Woods era: some governments have chosen external policy convergence by joining the "fixed" exchange regimes set up in Western Europe since the early 1970s, and other governments have retained domestic policy autonomy by avoiding any de jure exchange rate commitments. But I will show how the choice for external policy convergence or domestic policy autonomy is only weakly reflected in the exchange rate commitments and noncommitments of OECD governments in the post–Bretton Woods era. This is true because such exchange rate regimes as the European Snake and the exchange rate mechanism of the European Monetary System (EMS) were relatively flexible institutions, permitting substantial domestic monetary autonomy if member states so desired to assert it. Similarly, governments outside these exchange rate regimes could achieve relative exchange rate stability if they were willing to make the fiscal and monetary choices consistent with this external policy goal.

After discussing the evidence of policy—including monetary policy—divergence after 1973, I will address the second research question. What factors led national governments to choose domestic policy autonomy, accepting the loss of exchange rate stability with international capital mobility? Similarly, what factors pushed other national governments to move toward external policy convergence for greater exchange rate stability, sacrificing the benefits of domestic policy autonomy with international capital mobility?

My statistical analysis of government spending, national interest rates, interest rate differentials, and exchange rate variability point to the importance of the partisan character of the government in power. Leftist governments in the OECD have tended to spend more, hold higher nominal interest rates with larger interest rate differentials, and experience greater exchange rate variability than rightist governments, who tend toward the choices associated with external policy convergence. This suggests that many leftist governments have effectively chosen domestic policy autonomy with international capital mobility, while rightist governments have moved more toward exchange rate stability. The statistical models also show how political power-sharing arrangements have pushed OECD governments toward greater fiscal expansion and exchange rate variability, while central bank independence has helped them to reduce nominal interest rates and interest rate differentials.

To illustrate this partisan divergence with regard to the trade-off between domestic policy autonomy and exchange rate stability in the post–Bretton Woods era, I will employ two detailed case examples. The first shows how Socialist governments in France effectively opted for domestic policy autonomy even after Mitterrand's so-called U-turn in 1983. While in power, the Socialists maintained relatively high levels of government spending. With the international capital mobility constraint, this expansionary fiscal policy required higher national interest rates and larger interest rate differentials for the French national economy. Such a policy mix meant that the French franc was relatively unstable, even within the exchange rate mechanism of the EMS. Certainly, the Socialists could have cut government spending to achieve greater monetary convergence and reduce external currency variability, but they chose not to follow this strategy. While French policy independence imposed certain costs, the Socialists were willing to bear these costs for domestic political reasons.

The second case study shows how Conservative governments in Britain effectively chose external policy convergence for greater exchange rate stability, even while they remained outside of European exchange rate regimes. To achieve greater exchange rate stability, the Conservatives cut government spending. This allowed lower interest rates and smaller interest rate differentials for the British economy, helping to reduce external currency variability. This choice for external policy convergence also imposed costs on certain segments of British society, but the Conservatives were willing to pay these costs given the political support that they received from internationally oriented segments of the British economy, who desired exchange rate stability with international capital mobility.

These two examples function as least-likely cases, following Eckstein (1975). If we think about monetary policy divergence simply in terms of a government's de jure exchange rate regime commitments, we might reason that the French Socialists chose external policy convergence, since they were inside the EMS. We might also reason that the British Conservatives chose domestic policy autonomy, since they stayed outside of the EMS, except for a brief period in the early 1990s. But when we look carefully at the domestic fiscal and monetary policy choices made by these governments, we can better understand why the French Socialists had relatively unstable exchange rates within the flexible EMS regime and why the British Conservatives were able to achieve surprisingly stable exchange rates outside it.

3. Theoretical and Empirical Significance

The significance of this research project is threefold, and each of the three contributions addresses a different target audience. First, the research lays out clearly why the monetary convergence hypothesis is theoretically misleading and empirically wrong. It might be argued that such a demonstration is unnecessary, since many scholars, notably those in the field of comparative political economy (CPE), never really believed the argument in the first place. But many other scholars, especially in the field of international political economy (IPE), have seemingly accepted the logic of systematic monetary convergence.[8] It is

---

8. I suspect that IPE scholars have been more willing than their CPE counterparts to accept the monetary convergence hypothesis, because the basic argument builds from structural constraints on unit-level behavior, a logic with deep roots in the international relations tradition (see, e.g., Waltz 1979). One important exception in the IPE literature, arguing against the convergence hypothesis, is Oatley's 1999 article. Comparativists, trained to focus on unit-level differences, have appeared more willing to recognize policy divergence among national political economies; see, for example, Clark and Hallerberg 2000.

thus valuable to demonstrate, once and for all, why this "conventional wisdom" (Crystal 2004, 467) cannot be supported with regard to national monetary policy, the issue area that arguably represents the strongest case for the macroeconomic policy convergence argument.

Second, in uniting fiscal, monetary, and exchange rate policy into a common theoretical framework, this research project offers a new understanding of partisan economic differences in the capitalist global economy. If the first point is of little interest to CPE scholars, this second point should offer much greater appeal to this research community, because partisan models of national economic policy-making have recently come under strong attack (see, e.g., Clark 2003). It is thus useful to demonstrate how partisan arguments can be revived using a somewhat different and adapted theoretical framework.

Third, this policy mix framework also offers a new way to apply the Mundell-Fleming model to the context of domestic economic policy-making. Scholars of monetary politics in both the IPE and CPE traditions have tended to treat a country's exchange rate regime (usually categorized as either fixed or floating) as exogenously determined. But the policy mix framework explicitly makes exchange rate stability into an endogenous policy outcome, thus providing a framework that scholars may find useful in addressing the observed gap between de jure and de facto exchange rate regimes (see, e.g., Reinhart and Rogoff 2004; Levy-Yeyati and Sturzenegger 2005).

On the first point, speaking to those in the field of international relations, this research shows how and why monetary policy convergence is not inevitable with international capital mobility and global financial integration. This conclusion, however, does not mean that policy convergence could not occur due to deliberate choices on the part of national governments. But if it emerges from deliberate government choices, policy convergence is likely reversible when new governments, with different ideological perspectives and representing different societal interests, make purposeful choices for fiscal and monetary policy autonomy and accept the associated costs with regard to exchange rate stability.

This understanding bears on the familiar "agent-structure debate" in the field of international relations. Capital mobility is often treated as a structural condition of the international system,[9] thought to impose substantial constraints on national governments, the main agents in the international system. Especially with regard to international monetary politics, the debate thus far—dominated by the monetary convergence hypothesis—has been structure-heavy and agency-thin. The evidence presented in this book strengthens the

9. See Andrews 1994b; Webb 1995.

case for domestic economic agency, without denying the structural constraint of international capital mobility. International capital mobility certainly imposes some real constraints on national governments, leading them to pursue similar domestic policy goals, such as economic growth with low inflation. But national governments nonetheless retain a significant measure of political agency, since they can use different policy instruments—when properly coordinated—to meet these economic policy goals. This helps explain more precisely how international capital mobility constrains domestic economic policy-making: it constrains governments in terms of policy goals but not in terms of the policy instruments used to meet these goals.

This logic leads to the second contribution of this research project: establishing a new framework for understanding partisan politics with international capital mobility. To explain economic policy divergence in the post–Bretton Woods era, I will show some important partisan differences, at least with regard to the choice for domestic policy autonomy versus exchange rate stability. However, my partisan argument is a nuanced one, and I do not suggest that we should expect to observe partisan differences in terms of all economic policy choices and outcomes. To the contrary, while my theory of economic policy-making under international capital mobility predicts and finds partisan differences in terms of government spending (namely, government consumption), nominal interest rates, national interest rate differentials, and exchange rate variability, it also posits that we should not expect strong partisan differences in many other areas.

For example, if leftist governments balance greater spending with more tax revenue, then we should not expect to see significant partisan differences with regard to either budget deficits or public debt. Similarly, for reasons that will be discussed in later chapters, we should not expect to observe significant partisan differences in terms of real interest rates, actual inflation rates, or economic growth rates. Thus, my theory of partisan economic differences situates itself between those presented by Garrett (1995, 1998b), who argued for growing partisan differences on a wide variety of economic indicators, and Clark (2003), who argued that there are no significant partisan economic differences at all.

The third contribution of this project addresses political scientists studying the observed gap between de jure and de facto exchange rate regimes, a growing area of research in political economy. Central to this research program is the Mundell-Fleming framework imported from open-economy macroeconomics. So far, political science applications of the Mundell-Fleming framework to the context of domestic economic policy-making tend to begin with a country's exogenously determined exchange rate regime (assumed to be either fixed or floating) in order to explain its single "effective" domestic policy instrument—either fiscal policy with fixed exchange rates or monetary policy given a floating regime (see, e.g., Oatley 1999; Clark and Hallerberg 2000; Clark 2002).

While this is a very reasonable application of the Mundell-Fleming framework, it does have certain limitations, especially for the aforementioned research program. First, the approach tends to treat exchange rate regimes as one of two types, either fixed or floating. But until the introduction of the euro in 1999, OECD national economies have had neither truly fixed exchange rates nor purely floating ones in the post–Bretton Woods era. Most advanced industrial democracies, as well as most developing countries, have been somewhere in the muddy middle—between adjustable pegs and managed floats. Second, and more important, this approach treats a policy outcome (i.e., exchange rate stability) that the discipline is now trying to explain as exogenous. Furthermore, it does so generally in terms of the country's de jure exchange rate regime, a variable that has been shown in practice to be only weakly correlated with de facto exchange rate stability.

However, the policy mix framework presented in the present study directly addresses the issue of exchange rate stability, or de facto exchange rate regimes. It begins with the government's spending choice and nominal interest rate decision, showing how this combination, or policy mix, affects national exchange rate stability, effectively treating the country's de facto exchange rate regime as an endogenously determined variable. This direction of reasoning (from policy instruments to exchange rate stability) may help explain the surprisingly low correlation between exchange rate "words and deeds" (Levy-Yeyati and Sturzenegger 2005). If a government makes a fixed exchange rate commitment but then follows a fiscal and monetary policy mix expected to increase interest rate differentials and exacerbate external currency variability, we can better understand why the government's commitment to fix national exchange rates will be very hard, if not impossible, to achieve. Likewise, we can better understand how a government without any formal exchange rate commitments can achieve relatively stable exchange rates: it has chosen a fiscal and monetary policy mix that minimizes the national interest rate differential, thus reducing external currency variability.

4. The Organization of This Book

This book proceeds with six additional chapters. In this introductory chapter, I have presented the research questions and outlined my answers to them.

Chapter 2 ("The Monetary Convergence Hypothesis") develops the theoretical foundations for this project, including the Mundell-Fleming framework from open-economy macroeconomics and the systematic monetary convergence hypothesis from the field of international political economy.

Chapter 3 ("Evidence of Monetary Divergence") first offers and then validates some new operational measures for evaluating external monetary policy convergence and domestic monetary policy autonomy. Using these measures, I demonstrate that many, but certainly not all, OECD countries have maintained domestic monetary autonomy in the post–Bretton Woods era, thus producing a situation of monetary policy divergence (as opposed to monetary policy convergence) after 1973. Chapter 4 ("From Fiscal to Monetary Divergence") shows how this situation of monetary policy divergence is related to the well-documented phenomenon of OECD fiscal policy divergence in the post–Bretton Woods era. This chapter builds a theory based on the government's chosen fiscal and monetary policy mix, uniting differences in relative government spending to differences concerning nominal interest rates and exchange rate variability.

Given such policy divergence after 1973, chapter 5 ("Explaining Divergence in the Policy Mix") explores the determinants of domestic policy autonomy and exchange rate variability among the OECD countries in the post–Bretton Woods era. The statistical results show the importance of the partisan character of the government in power with regard to government spending, nominal interest rates, interest rate differentials, and exchange rate variability. Chapter 6 ("Illustrating Partisan Divergence in the Policy Mix") further demonstrates the importance of government partisanship through two detailed case examples: the example of the French Socialists from 1981 to 1995 and the example of the British Conservatives from 1979 to 1996.

Finally, chapter 7 ("Expanding the Argument") discusses the broader theoretical and policy implications of this research. In particular, it shows how the pressures for domestic policy autonomy are likely to reemerge within Europe's Economic and Monetary Union (EMU). With such pressures, it may be hard to sustain the EMU project unless member states can reacquire some lost policy autonomy, especially on the fiscal side. But at the same time, greater fiscal policy independence within the Eurozone will make it harder for the new regional central bank to set a common European monetary policy. Consequently, the EMU project may rest on more fragile foundations than many observers seem willing to acknowledge.

CHAPTER 2

The Monetary Convergence Hypothesis

The first research puzzle at the focus of this book concerns the hypothesis of systematic monetary policy convergence among the advanced industrial democracies in the post–Bretton Woods era. In what is arguably its most favorable theoretical domain, can we observe much evidence of monetary policy convergence and the corresponding loss of domestic monetary autonomy? To answer this question, it is important to lay out—in much greater detail than was possible in the introductory chapter—the monetary convergence proposition. It is also important to define some major concepts that will be used throughout the book.

This chapter begins with a simple presentation of the macroeconomic model known as the Mundell-Fleming framework. For readers well acquainted with the model, this may be an unnecessary presentation, and they are urged to skip ahead. For many other readers, it will help to define some important conceptual issues.

As I mentioned in chapter 1 and will further demonstrate in this chapter, systematic monetary policy convergence is a curious proposition. While it has not yet been convincingly demonstrated, a large number of political scientists (but certainly not all) seemingly accept the basic hypothesis. I suspect that some of this acceptance may simply stem from conceptual confusion. Occasionally in print and more often in conversation, one encounters the tendency to treat the terms *international capital mobility* and *monetary policy convergence* as effective synonyms. Perhaps this development is not surprising since the terms *financial market integration* (a common term for expressing international capital mobility) and *monetary integration* (an alternative phrase for monetary policy convergence) sound similar. But treating these terms as equivalent is not only misleading but technically incorrect.

On this point, the Mundell-Fleming framework helps demonstrate how international capital mobility is conceptually distinct from monetary policy convergence, or the loss of domestic monetary autonomy. The former concept concerns private capital markets, while the latter is concerned with how public sector actors use the national monetary policy instrument. Thus, we simply cannot take the well-established fact of international capital mobility among the advanced industrial democracies in the post–Bretton Woods era as prima facie evidence for their monetary policy convergence. Not only are international capital mobility and systematic monetary policy convergence different theoretical concepts, the former is not even a sufficient condition for the latter.

After presenting the Mundell-Fleming framework, this chapter will work through the logic of the monetary convergence hypothesis as it has been developed in the political science literature. This exercise helps demonstrate how the hypothesis has advanced in the discipline, despite the lack of strong empirical evidence supporting the theoretical proposition. Of course, that there is not yet much evidence in favor of systematic monetary convergence does not mean that the hypothesis is falsified. But it does reveal how the hypothesis desperately requires some rigorous empirical evaluation.

Finally, having worked through the details of the monetary convergence hypothesis, this chapter will conclude by discussing several problems facing its causal logic. These potential problems illustrate why we cannot continue to accept the notion of systematic monetary convergence among the advanced industrial democracies in the post–Bretton Woods era without bringing some additional evidence to bear on the proposition. Such evidence is presented in chapter 3.

1. The Mundell-Fleming Framework

The model known in the open-economy macroeconomic literature as the Mundell-Fleming framework (Mundell 1960, 1963, 1968; Fleming 1962) is perhaps more commonly known in the political science literature as the "unholy trinity" (Cohen 1993) or "impossible trinity" (Broz and Frieden 2001). At its most basic level, the model describes the existence of a monetary policy trilemma facing national policymakers. This monetary trilemma states that from a menu of three potentially desirable economic conditions—(1) domestic monetary policy autonomy, (2) external currency stability, and (3) international capital mobility—governments can achieve at most only two of the three at any one time.

The first menu item—domestic monetary policy autonomy—simply refers to the ability of national governments to direct their monetary policy instrument toward certain domestic economic objectives. For example, faced with an economic decline and societal demands for more growth and employment, governments might desire to lower interest rates to stimulate economic activity. Alternatively, in an economy with rising prices and societal demands for domestic price stability, governments might like to raise interest rates to reduce inflationary pressures. While there are certainly limits to what governments may be able to achieve domestically with interest rate changes, especially if market actors anticipate such changes in advance, democratic governments nonetheless perceive monetary policy independence as potentially desirable in at least the short to medium term.

The second menu item—external currency stability—is defined as fixing the national currency's value relative to some external benchmark. Many actors consider exchange rate stability as desirable because currency variability and volatility potentially impede cross-border trade and investment. Indeed, governments often cite expanding international trade and, by extension, national income as the major justification for making fixed exchange rate commitments. For example, a positive relationship between exchange rate stability and international trade was given as the main foundation for monetary coordination leading to monetary union in Western Europe (see, e.g., Commission of the European Communities 1990).[1]

At this point, it is also useful to distinguish between a country's de jure and de facto exchange rate regimes. The former refers to the formal, or stated, commitments made by the government, often to fix or stabilize the national exchange rate within a certain range. The latter refers to the actual stability of the national currency's value relative to some external benchmark. Governments that achieve greater external currency stability are said to have a more fixed de facto exchange rate regime. Thus, the second menu item—external currency stability—is a synonym for de facto fixity, which may be unrelated, in practice, to de jure regimes and commitments. This is a very important point, which will be discussed in more detail later in this chapter.

The third menu item—international capital mobility—refers to the ability of investors to move their money and capital assets across international bor-

1. Despite the expected connection between exchange rate stability and increased cross-border commerce, it is important to acknowledge that the evidence on this relationship is, at best, mixed. As one International Monetary Fund review reported: "The large majority of empirical studies on the impact of exchange rate variability on the volume of international trade are unable to establish a systematically significant link between measured exchange rate variability and the volume of international trade, whether on an aggregated or on a bilateral basis" (cited from Edison and Melvin 1990, 21). Similarly, Levy-Yeyati and Sturzenegger (2003) found no link between de facto fixed exchange rates and economic growth for developed countries.

ders without government interference. National governments arguably prize international capital mobility because of the efficiency gains associated with integrated financial markets. Capital abundance is a desirable economic condition, and an open financial market serves to attract capital assets from outside the domestic economy. Furthermore, regulating national capital markets became a difficult task for democratic governments beginning in the late 1960s. As Krugman (1999, 61) argued, governments want "to assure business that money can be freely moved in or out of the country, if only to avoid the bureaucracy, paperwork, and opportunities for corruption inevitably associated with any attempt to limit capital movements."

There is, of course, a potential downside to international capital mobility. Open financial markets also allow for capital assets to exit the domestic economy when local conditions become less attractive relative to external investment opportunities. Thus, of the three menu items of the "impossible trinity," international capital mobility may be the least prized by national governments. Cohen (1993, 147) observed, "if polled 'off the record' for their private preferences, however, most [governments] would probably admit to prizing exchange-rate stability and policy autonomy even more [than international capital mobility]."

Since governments can choose only two of these three menu items at any one time, the Mundell-Fleming trilemma identifies the possibility of three different international monetary orientations. These three different international monetary orientations, or combinations of monetary policy choices, are concisely illustrated in figure 1. At least in principle, governments could be at any of the three sides of the triangle; but at any given side, they lose the desirable economic condition at the opposite angle. Over the last century, we have certainly seen examples of all three international monetary policy orientations, as illustrated in figure 2. For convenience reasons, scholars have often tended to identify a dominant international monetary orientation with a particular historical period, although such characterizations do not necessarily mean that all governments in the international monetary system necessarily followed the dominant orientation during the period in question.[2]

Political scientists have also sometimes talked as if international capital mobility is a relatively new feature of the international monetary system, unique to the post–Bretton Woods era. But international capital mobility

2. For example, Cohen (1995, 212) notes that even during the classic gold standard, supposedly the golden age of exchange rate stability under capital mobility, "monetary authorities developed a variety of techniques for evading the rules of the game." He adds, "Monetary policies in this period were never really either fully passive or simply automatic."

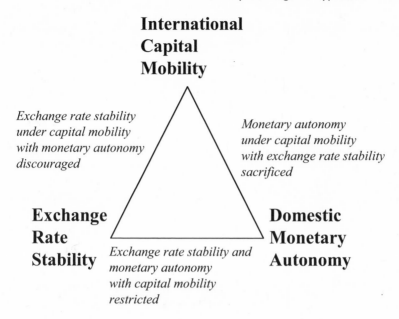

International Capital Mobility

Exchange rate stability under capital mobility with monetary autonomy discouraged

Monetary autonomy under capital mobility with exchange rate stability sacrificed

Exchange Rate Stability

Exchange rate stability and monetary autonomy with capital mobility restricted

Domestic Monetary Autonomy

Fig. I.   Three International Monetary Policy Orientations

marked the years before World War I, as well as the interwar era (see Verdier 1998; Nurkse 1944). To protect against external currency variability, the major powers in the international system constructed "fixed" exchange rate regimes, the successful operation of which required the subordination of monetary policy to the external objective of maintaining a stable currency. The classic gold standard, which operated between 1870 until the outbreak of World War I, is generally considered a success in terms of exchange rate stability (see, e.g., Gilpin 1987, 123–27), in large part because governments had not yet developed the interventionist practices—requiring domestic policy autonomy—that would later come to characterize the Keynesian welfare state (Ruggie 1982).

After World War I, the European powers attempted to construct another fixed exchange rate regime under the condition of international capital mobility. However, the new gold exchange standard, adopted in 1922, was only partially successful in stabilizing national exchange rates (see Simmons 1996). During the interwar years, European governments faced better-organized domestic constituencies and new political ideologies demanding that available policy instruments be directed toward internal economic objectives (see Eichengreen 1996, chap. 3). Under such political pressure, the gold exchange

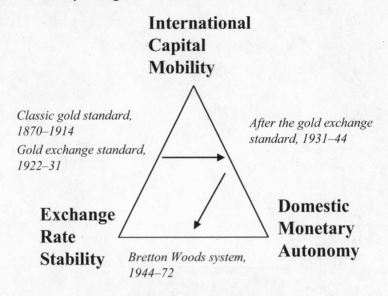

International Capital Mobility

Classic gold standard, 1870–1914

Gold exchange standard, 1922–31

After the gold exchange standard, 1931–44

Exchange Rate Stability

Bretton Woods system, 1944–72

Domestic Monetary Autonomy

Fig. 2.   Examples of Different International Monetary Orientations

standard was abandoned in the early 1930s, as national governments opted for domestic policy autonomy under international capital mobility, sacrificing the external goal of exchange rate stability.

The Bretton Woods system, created in 1944 and ended in the early 1970s, sought to provide national governments with both external currency stability and domestic policy autonomy. Ruggie (1982) labeled this new international monetary orientation "embedded liberalism," since the Bretton Woods system was economically liberal, seeking to foster international trade with more stable exchange rates. The fixed exchange rate regime in operation during the Bretton Woods era pegged the value of the U.S. dollar to gold and then pegged other national currencies to the U.S. dollar. But this internationally liberal orientation was embedded in a larger framework that permitted and even encouraged governments to intervene in their domestic economies to achieve national (and partisan) objectives concerning economic growth, employment, and inflation.

To obtain exchange rate stability with domestic monetary policy autonomy, governments were forced to restrict international capital flows, as much as it was possible to do so. Indeed, the Bretton Woods agreement acknowledged the right of states to impose capital controls and financial restrictions designed to discourage speculative flows of money (i.e., capital movements not linked to trade flows). John Maynard Keynes (quoted from Gold 1977, 11) explained: "As a permanent arrangement, the plan accords to every member government the explicit right to control all capital movements. What used to be heresy is now endorsed as orthodox. . . . It follows that our right to control the domestic capital market is secured on firmer foundations than ever before, and is formally accepted as a proper part of agreed international agreements."

But restricting international capital flows was easier said than done. To cite Cohen's "Iron Law of Economic Controls," "limits on capital mobility must be multiplied at a rate at least equal to that at which means are found to circumvent them" (Cohen 1993, 147). In fact, the current and capital accounts of many advanced industrial democracies were quite open during the 1960s, before the final end of the Bretton Woods system in the early 1970s (see Quinn and Inclan 1997). With the expanding ability of capital holders to move their assets across national borders, governments simply could not simultaneously maintain both a fixed exchange rate and domestic policy autonomy. One or the other had to be sacrificed; consequently, the Bretton Woods system ended.

As I mentioned earlier, financial integration among the advanced industrial democracies has only expanded further in the post–Bretton Woods era. Consequently, I accept the conclusion advanced by other scholars (see Andrews 1994b; Webb 1995) that international capital mobility can reasonably be treated as a structural feature of the international monetary system, at least in the global North. Even if certain governments, especially rightist ones, encouraged capital liberalization (see Helleiner 1994), the international capital mobility constraint has become extremely difficult to reverse, even for leftist governments, due to advances in information and communications technology, as well as changes in national regulatory environments and market practices (see Bryant 1987; Cerny 1993; Goodman and Pauly 1993). Andrews (1994b, 214) has persuasively concluded: "the difficulties in reversing the trend toward financial integration derive in part from this diversity of sources and in part from their collective interaction. The costs of reversing the technological advances that underlie capital mobility are difficult to contemplate in any straightforward counterfactual sense."

Thus, at least for the advanced industrial democracies in the post–Bretton Woods era, the Mundell-Fleming trilemma can be reduced to a simpler dilemma. This dilemma concerns the trade-off between external currency stability and domestic monetary policy autonomy. Understanding this monetary policy trade-off in the post–Bretton Woods era brings us to the second research puzzle explored in this book. What factors have led the advanced industrial democracies to choose exchange rate stability, and what factors led them instead toward domestic monetary autonomy under the condition of international capital mobility?

2. The Systematic Monetary Convergence Hypothesis

As I mentioned earlier, many political scientists, especially in the field of international political economy, would argue that we can already answer the question posed at the end of the preceding section. They propose that pressures associated with international capital mobility, or globally integrated financial markets, have made domestic monetary policy autonomy unachievable for the advanced industrial democracies in the post–Bretton Woods era. They thus maintain that, albeit with differing degrees of enthusiasm, OECD governments have been forced to make low inflation their overriding economic policy objective, which has led them toward exchange rate stability and away from domestic monetary autonomy (see fig. 3). Evidence supporting this proposition can arguably be seen in the various multilateral "fixed" exchange rate regimes formed in Western Europe since the early 1970s: first the European Snake (1972–78), followed by the European Monetary System (1979–98), and now the Economic and Monetary Union (since 1999). While not all OECD governments joined these multilateral regimes, many outsiders made similar unilateral commitments to fix their exchange rates.

The preceding paragraph concisely summarizes what might be termed the systematic monetary convergence hypothesis, known also in political science literature as the "capital mobility hypothesis" (Andrews 1994b). As I mentioned in chapter 1, the broad macroeconomic policy convergence hypothesis first entered the political science literature in the early 1990s (see table 1). While various parts of the broad macroeconomic convergence hypothesis have been seriously challenged, especially with regard to fiscal policy, monetary convergence remains a widely accepted proposition in certain circles. Even scholars critical of the "globalization as policy constraint" research program have stated that monetary policy remains the strongest case for the macroeconomic policy convergence thesis (see, e.g., Garrett 1998a, 802; Drezner 2001, 75).

One of the earliest statements in support of systematic monetary policy convergence came from Goodman (1992), who concluded that international capital mobility has "increased the overall pressure for monetary convergence" (217) and that, consequently, the "assumption of autonomy has become increasingly less tenable" (221). The loss of domestic policy autonomy was supposed to be especially acute for smaller OECD countries, as Moses (1994,

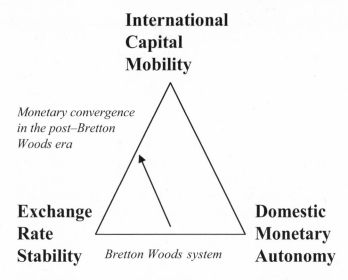

International
Capital
Mobility

Monetary convergence
in the post–Bretton
Woods era

Exchange   **Domestic**
Rate   **Monetary**
Stability   *Bretton Woods system*   **Autonomy**

Fig. 3.   The International Monetary Orientation Predicted by the
Systematic Monetary Policy Convergence Hypothesis

133) argued: "In a world with capital mobility, this has required that monetary policy [be] aimed at defending the exchange rate, and can no longer be used for internal stabilization. In effect, these changes have created a policy dilemma, limiting the number of policy instruments available to small open economies. Those that do remain appear to be insufficient for maintaining both internal and external balances." Moses continued, "instruments that were traditionally used for managing the internal balance have been diverted away from the internal balance and used to defend the external balance" (135), including the exchange rate.

Webb (1994) broadened this conclusion beyond just the small open economies, writing that "[w]ith few exceptions, national policy making autonomy has eroded dramatically" (395) and that "states—even the largest—have lost a great deal of macroeconomic . . . autonomy because of the growth of capital mobility" (399). Andrews (1994a, 428) reached a similar conclusion: "as a general proposition, the degree of variation in monetary policy among different states has observably narrowed during the past fifteen or so years. One fundamental, underlying reason for this change has been the heightened external constraint imposed upon states by international financial integration." Similarly, Milner and Keohane (1996, 248) concluded that "internationalization, especially in the form of capital mobility, reduces the autonomy and efficacy of governments' macroeconomic policy choices."

Using stronger language, Cerny (1995, 612) argued that "globalization has undercut the policy capacity of the national state in all but a few areas." These remaining areas certainly do not include monetary policy, as "currency exchange rates and interest rates are increasingly set in globalizing market-places, and governments attempt to manipulate them at their peril" (ibid., 609). Perhaps the strongest statement about the loss of domestic monetary autonomy came from Ohmae (1995, 12), who wrote: "as the workings of gen-uinely global capital markets dwarf their ability to control exchange rates or protect their currency, nation states have become inescapably vulnerable to the disciple imposed by economic choices made elsewhere by people and institu-tions over which they have no practical control." As such, he continued, "the nation state is increasingly a nostalgic fiction."[3]

As readers should now understand after working through the Mundell-Fleming framework, international capital mobility does not necessarily mean the loss of domestic monetary autonomy, although it is a necessary condition. Oatley (1997, 15–16) correctly noted in his review of the monetary conver-gence literature: "even if we treat a high level of capital mobility as exogenously given, we are still left with the need to explain which of the remaining two [menu items, exchange rate stability or domestic monetary policy autonomy] will be chosen." To explain this choice, IPE scholars often argued that the costs associated with exchange rate instability and volatility were simply too high for OECD governments and their capitalist supporters to bear. Andrews (1994a, 428) wrote about the Western European experience in this regard, noting a strong regional "predisposition towards exchange rate stability." Webb (1991, 318) advanced an even broader argument, writing that "governments are not willing to tolerate the drastic exchange rate fluctuations that accompany mon-etary policy choices which reflect only domestic concerns." He continued, "The high costs of exchange rate volatility mean that, despite economic theory, international capital mobility does *not* increase the real-world effectiveness of monetary policy" (319).[4]

---

3. I include so many quotations by prominent scholars in an effort to demonstrate that mon-etary policy convergence with the loss of domestic policy autonomy is not a "straw man" hypoth-esis. To the contrary, these quotes (and many others that I do not reproduce here) show how this hypothesis was forcefully advanced by IPE scholars in the 1990s. Indeed, this literature continues to be cited by IPE scholars as evidence of macroeconomic policy convergence.

4. It is important to acknowledge that many of the scholars cited here were not trying to explain exchange rate stability per se; instead, they were more interested in OECD inflation con-vergence. In this regard, exchange rate stability and low inflation are different policy outcomes, a

Indeed, the first wave of literature on the policy constraints imposed by globalization went beyond the loss of monetary autonomy, often including the loss of fiscal autonomy (see, e.g., Scharpf 1991; Kurzer 1993). With neither fiscal nor monetary policy instruments at their immediate disposal, it was often argued that leftist and rightist political parties, once in power, would have to govern the national economy in a very similar manner. We should thus expect to observe partisan economic policy convergence in the post–Bretton Woods era. Garrett and Lange (1991, 543) summarized, "in anything but the short run, the fiscal and monetary policies of governments of the left and the right should converge." More specifically, convergence was expected to occur on the economic policies and outcomes favored by the political right—notably, reduced government spending, lower inflation, and more stable exchange rates. Kurzer (1993, 3) further argued, while "social democratic parties are again or still in power, . . . they simply follow the cues and programs of right-wing or conservative parties and have no alternatives to proposals to shrink the public sector, privatize social services, and deregulate labor markets."

By the mid-1990s, the hypothesis that economic globalization including international capital mobility was forcing OECD governments of the political left and right to constrain government spending and limiting their fiscal policy choices came under strong attack in the second wave of political science literature on the subject (see table 1). If anything, average OECD government spending relative to the gross domestic product has expanded since the early 1970s,[5] consistent with the growth in international capital mobility. Scholars now debate whether this rise in relative government spending stems more from greater economic openness including international capital mobility (see Garrett 1995, 1998b) or from deindustrialization unrelated to it (see Iversen and Cusack 2000). Although there are arguably no definitive conclusions, the second-wave debate successfully demonstrated how little evidence exists to support the conclusion that international capital mobility has forced systematic cuts in OECD government expenditures across a wide range of spending cate-

---

point that I will develop in later chapters. Unfortunately, the two outcomes have become very closely linked in the minds of many IPE scholars, and this link is perhaps reinforced by arguments from economics that exchange rates should stabilize as national inflation rates converge (according to the model of purchasing power parity) and that fixing the exchange rate may be a solution to the problem of domestic inflation. Indeed, on many IPE syllabi, the literature on OECD capital mobility and inflation convergence is situated right next to the literature on fixed exchange rate regimes. The close proximity of these two arguments (international capital mobility and fixed exchange rates) has certainly encouraged acceptance of the monetary policy convergence hypothesis, even if many of the original scholars did not intend to make precisely this argument. I thank Michael Webb for making this point clear to me.

5. For evidence on this point, see Garrett 1998a, 813; 1998b, 77.

gories (see Burgoon 2001), even if certain advanced industrial democracies have made deliberate choices for fiscal contraction.

But this second wave of literature barely considered the original hypothesis of monetary policy convergence and the related issue of exchange rate stability.[6] On this point, Drezner (2001, 65) observed a "paucity" of empirical studies concerning the policy convergence hypothesis in a number of important issue areas. As further evidence on this point, it is notable that the growing literature on the varieties of capitalism (see, e.g., Kitschelt et al. 1999; Hall and Soskice 2001) tends to focus almost exclusively on national differences with regard to welfare spending, taxation, and regulatory policy without addressing in depth the topic of divergent national monetary policy choices. The unwillingness or inability to test the monetary convergence hypothesis may stem in part from the fact that while it is relatively easy to obtain reliable data on government spending and other fiscal policy indicators, it has been much harder to identify good operational measures for the loss of domestic monetary policy autonomy and corresponding stability of national exchange rates. Thus, the hypothesis of systematic monetary policy convergence has remained largely untested.

This development (or lack thereof) does not mean that all political scientists currently accept the monetary convergence hypothesis. Clearly, some never believed the argument from the outset; for example, Oatley (1999) and Clark and Hallerberg (2000) presented early evidence in support of monetary policy divergence. Other scholars rejected international capital mobility as the real cause for the loss of monetary policy autonomy, but they did so without explicitly rejecting the phenomenon of monetary policy convergence in Western Europe and elsewhere. Thus, we have reached the third wave of literature on the subject, which offers new explanations for monetary cooperation and integration, concepts that are clearly related to the original idea of monetary policy convergence and the corresponding loss of domestic monetary autonomy (see table 1). For example, McNamara (1998, 2) proposed that a new policy consensus on neoliberal economic ideas can explain why "political actors from socialist to conservative [have] supported an exchange rate regime that in effect gives away economic policy tools and limits their ability to use macroeconomic policy to distinguish themselves [to groups in society]."

---

6. Garrett's work (1995; 1998b) considered the effect of internationalization on national interest rates, but monetary policy was not his primary focus, and he seems to have read his results as being generally consistent with the monetary convergence hypothesis. Finding that an interest rate premium has been imposed on leftist governments who engage in greater fiscal policy expansion, Garrett (1995, 683) speculated that "[i]n time . . . no government would be able to bear this burden."

At this point in time, it is perhaps tempting to believe that the discipline has moved so far away from the original monetary convergence hypothesis that it is no longer necessary to investigate it empirically. But it seems that the proposition may be on the verge of making a comeback, based on new arguments originating in the field of international economics. For example, Calvo and Reinhart (2002) have described a "fear of floating" phenomenon that leads governments without any formal commitments to fix their exchange rate (i.e., de jure floaters) to behave as de facto fixers. Likewise, Frankel, Schmukler, and Serven (2002) have argued that only the very largest countries can obtain the benefits associated with monetary policy independence. Their empirical work, while strongly criticized by Shambaugh (2004), suggests that monetary policy autonomy is effectively disappearing in most regions of the globe, not just in Western Europe.

Thus, it seems inadequate to say that nobody currently believes in monetary policy convergence so the hypothesis does not require any testing. Many scholars continue to accept the proposition. Furthermore, they do so despite a number of theoretical and empirical problems that I will briefly outline in the next section of this chapter.

3. Problems with the Monetary Convergence Hypothesis

The first problem facing the monetary convergence hypothesis concerns the nature of "fixed" exchange rates in the post–Bretton Woods era. As evidence of external monetary policy convergence, political scientists often point to the fact that many governments in Western Europe have participated in a series of multilateral monetary and exchange rate regimes since the early 1970s: first the European Snake, then the European Monetary System (EMS), and now the Economic and Monetary Union (EMU). Furthermore, other OECD governments, not directly participating in these regimes, made similar unilateral commitments to "fix" the value of their national currency.

Putting aside for a moment this evidence's limited cross-sectional domain (restricted to only Western Europe), membership in these multilateral currency regimes can be treated as persuasive evidence of external monetary convergence and the corresponding loss of domestic monetary autonomy if—and only if—it can be demonstrated that these monetary commitments have operated as de facto fixed exchange rate regimes, thus significantly constraining the policy choices of member governments with international capital mobility. On this point, the evidence is not particularly strong. Beginning with the European Snake, most observers (see, e.g., Gros and Thygesen 1992; Ungerer 1997; McNamara 1998, chap. 5) have written off this first regional monetary institution as weak and almost completely ineffective in promoting regional exchange rate stability.

Other scholars, including McNamara (1998, chaps. 6–7), have written in more positive terms about the European Snake's successor, the exchange rate mechanism of the European Monetary System. But even if it was associated with less exchange rate variability than the European Snake, the EMS hardly qualifies as a truly fixed exchange rate regime. Its exchange rate mechanism permitted the exchange rates of member states to fluctuate within fairly wide bands as compared to the more fixed Bretton Woods system.[7] Furthermore, when national governments could not maintain their currency values within those bands, the band limits could be realigned, permitting additional domestic monetary autonomy. For such reasons, even optimistic assessments of the EMS characterized the arrangement as "more akin to a crawling peg" than to a fixed exchange rate regime (Froot and Rogoff 1991, 270). Consistent with this view, Ungerer (1997, 174) documented eighteen major realignment events within the EMS from 1979 to 1995, involving more than fifty separate national currency adjustments. Certainly, these realignments became less frequent in the 1990s. But this fact arguably stems less from the achievement of external monetary convergence and more from the decision to widen the EMS bands to 30 percent after the 1992 European exchange rate crisis, thus turning the exchange rate mechanism into something like a "managed float," where formal realignments to maintain the appearance of a "fix" were hardly necessary.

Perhaps the strongest evidence in favor of European monetary convergence emerged in the middle to late 1990s, as many governments in the region prepared for the Economic and Monetary Union, adopting convergence criteria of the 1992 Maastricht Agreement. By the end of 1997, preexisting national monetary and fiscal policy divergences had been reduced, paving the way for the new European regional currency and a common European monetary policy set by the new European Central Bank. But even with this more recent evidence in favor of regional monetary convergence, political scientists must exercise caution.

In retrospect, the late 1990s now appear as an unusual era of high economic

---

7. The Bretton Woods system had bands around a par value allowing a 2 percent fluctuation (plus or minus 1 percent). By contrast, the EMS band width for most member states was 4.5 percent (plus or minus 2.25 percent) until 1993. For member states needing greater flexibility (e.g., Italy), the band width was 12 percent. The three EMS latecomers (Britain, Spain, and Portugal) also used the wider bands, first negotiated by Italy. After 1993, the bands were further widened to 30 percent (plus or minus 15 percent). As Obstfeld and Rogoff (1995, 73) concluded, this was "a system barely distinguishable from floating."

growth and low inflation for most of the advanced industrial democracies. If the 1970s can be called a period of stagflation, when governments were simultaneously plagued by stagnant economies and high inflation, the late 1990s might be conversely treated as a period of noninflationary growth. With steady economic growth, tax revenues boomed, allowing governments to reduce their budget deficits and retire public debt (see Gobbin and Van Aarle 2001), often without any substantial cuts in government spending. The lack of corresponding price pressures also meant that the Maastricht inflation target became relatively easy to achieve, permitting nominal interest rates to fall in Europe, as in much of the rest of the global North. In fact, many advanced industrial democracies outside of Western Europe, including the United States, would have effectively satisfied the EMU fiscal and monetary convergence criteria, although there was neither political pressure to do so nor any opportunity to join the new institution. Von Hagen and Strauch (2001, 342) concluded, "There is . . . no need for a 'Maastricht effect' to explain these consolidations."

Von Hagen and Strauch's conclusion, echoed by others,[8] does not mean that some monetary policy convergence has not occurred. But it does suggest that recent policy convergence in Western Europe rests on a somewhat fragile foundation. As the 1990s boom ended and the region again experienced economic contraction with corresponding societal demands for domestic policy autonomy, several governments with EMU commitments found themselves pushing the fiscal limits set by the 1997 Stability and Growth Pact. Other EMU member states have expressed their dissatisfaction with the regional monetary policy set by the European Central Bank.[9] Finally, three EU member states (Britain, Sweden, and Denmark) have quite successfully run their national economies outside of the EMU arrangement, thus demonstrating the potential attractiveness and viability of domestic policy autonomy for European governments in the twenty-first century. Consequently, because several EU governments remain outside the institution and because many of those inside are behaving in a manner inconsistent with the rules for regional policy convergence, it is not reasonable to conclude that the EMU represents the final proof of Western European policy convergence. I will return to this point in chapter 7.

If—despite all the evidence to the contrary—political scientists still wish to insist that such European monetary regimes as the Snake and the EMS are con-

8. See also an unpublished paper by Ringe (2003) showing that success in meeting the various Maastricht convergence criteria can largely be explained by a business cycle model.

9. See, for example, *Economist* 2001b.

sistent with de facto exchange rate fixity, then they run up against a new problem regarding the monetary convergence hypothesis. This second problem
concerns its now ambiguous theoretical domain. If we treat membership in a
European multilateral currency regime as a strong indicator of monetary policy convergence, what can we say about the OECD governments in North
America and the Pacific, who have not created and participated in formal monetary regimes like those found in Western Europe? Can we reasonably conclude
that Western Europe has converged with regard to monetary policy but that
the other OECD governments in North America and the Pacific have not? If we
accept such a conclusion, what does this regional dichotomy say about the various possible explanations for monetary policy convergence?

In fact, it is very hard to square this empirical conclusion—that Western
Europe is monetary policy convergent while the other OECD governments are
not—with the major theoretical explanations advanced in the third wave of literature (see table 1 in chap. 1) to explain monetary cooperation and integration in Western Europe. McNamara (1998) put forth an explanation based on
neoliberal policy ideas, while Frieden (2002) updated his earlier argument
focusing on the political pressure applied by international exporters and
investors, who favor exchange rate stability. If these are indeed the major factors directly explaining monetary cooperation and exchange rate stability, then
we must acknowledge the power of neoliberal economic ideas in the non-European OECD countries, especially the United States and Japan.[10] Likewise, it
becomes necessary to recognize the political pressure that can be applied by
internationally oriented big business in every capitalist economy. These possible explanations for monetary policy convergence lead us toward the conclusion that it must be a broad OECD experience.[11] Yet the standard political science measure for monetary policy convergence—membership in a multilateral
currency regime, with nonmembership marking domestic policy autonomy—
leads us to a different conclusion: that policy convergence has been a uniquely
European phenomenon. Simply stated, it is hard to reconcile our currently
limited empirical evidence for monetary policy convergence with the theoretical explanations that have recently been advanced to explain it.

A third potential problem facing the monetary convergence hypothesis concerns these very theoretical explanations: the influence of neoliberal policy
ideas among statist actors and the growing political power exerted by societal
actors, such as international exporters and investors, who prefer monetary

10. The United States is regularly identified as a neoliberal political economy (see, e.g., Iversen
and Wren 1998). On the influence of neoliberal policy ideas in Japan, see Takenaka 1991.

11. This is true despite the fact that both McNamara and Frieden test their arguments only on
European cases.

integration and exchange rate stability. While McNamara (1998) and Frieden (2002) made very reasonable arguments about the potential influence of these factors, their empirical work does not discuss or include important counter-vailing policy ideas and societal political pressures.

Even if triumphing over Keynesian ideas in the 1980s, neoliberal policy ideas, drawn from monetarist economic theory and supposedly pushing governments toward external policy convergence, had to contend with major new policy ideas in the 1990s. The most notable new contender went by the name of endogenous growth—or new growth—theory.[12] This economic policy idea, which was especially influential within left-wing political circles (see Boix 1997, 1998), made novel arguments to justify state intervention in the national economy, provided that government spending was directed toward public investment projects including infrastructure, worker training, and research and development. Thus, just as certain ideas were pushing governments toward external policy convergence, other ideas were leading governments back toward fiscal expansion and associated domestic policy autonomy.

Likewise, even if international exporters and investors pressured governments for monetary integration and exchange rate stability, OECD governments also faced countervailing pressures for domestic policy autonomy from the nontradable service sector. Iversen, Wren, and Cusack (Iversen and Wren 1998; Iversen and Cusack 2000) have demonstrated the political influence of this domestically oriented economic sector in setting national economic priorities. Even if it does not have the same exit option afforded international investors, the service sector's large and growing economic size gives it a powerful voice in pushing democratic governments toward domestic policy autonomy and away from exchange rate stability.[13] In short, much the same logic concerning interest group pressures that has been used to explain external policy convergence could also be employed to explain domestic policy divergence. Indeed, I will do precisely this in chapter 5.

The fourth and final problem that the logic underlying the monetary convergence hypothesis must confront was mentioned in chapter 1. The second wave of scholarship on the effects of economic globalization and international capital mobility soundly rejected the proposition of fiscal policy convergence in the post–Bretton Woods era (see, e.g., Garrett 1995; Garrett 1998b; Kitschelt

---

12. On endogenous—or new growth—theory, see Aschauer 1990; Barro 1990; Romer 1990; Barro and Sala-I-Martin 1995; Alesina and Perotti 1996. For a concise summary, see Gilpin 2001, chap. 5.

13. On the size of the nontradable service sector, see the 1994 article by De Gregorio, Giovannini, and Wolf. Their evidence shows that services are not becoming more tradable. Hence, this sector would continue to hold preferences for domestic policy autonomy.

et al. 1999; Burgoon 2001; Hall and Soskice 2001). Although the details of fiscal policy divergence remain a source of scholarly disagreement, there is very little evidence that international capital mobility has forced OECD governments to cut taxes and spending, reduce deficits, and retire public debt, even if certain advanced industrial democracies have made such policy decisions. Thus, how can we sustain a story of monetary policy convergence next to all the evidence showing fiscal policy divergence among the advanced industrial democracies in the post–Bretton Woods era?

Perhaps if we can completely divorce monetary policy and interest rate decisions from those involving government spending and budget deficits, it will be possible to find convergence with regard to one policy instrument (monetary) and at the same time demonstrate divergence in the use of the other main policy instrument (fiscal). The notion of monetary policy convergence next to existing evidence of fiscal policy divergence might also be sustainable when employing a very simplified model of the national political economy—a model in which governments have only one policy goal, which can be satisfied using a single policy instrument. However, it is very difficult to build a reasonable model of national economic policy-making without acknowledging that governments have multiple policy goals but relatively few policy instruments through which to achieve their goals. Once we accept the idea that governments have multiple policy goals that cannot be satisfied simultaneously using a single policy instrument, we must confront the fact that governments may need to coordinate their limited number of policy instruments to target different economic objectives at the same time. Thus, fiscal policy differences at the national level could produce the situation of monetary policy divergence, defined to exist when governments move interest rates in different directions toward different economic objectives, depending on whether they contract or expand their fiscal policy instruments.

In conclusion, there are some very good reasons to question the hypothesis of OECD monetary policy convergence in the post–Bretton Woods era. Thus, we simply cannot continue to accept the monetary convergence proposition without more rigorous empirical testing. The task ahead in chapter 3 is to bring some additional evidence to bear on the proposition. If the hypothesis passes its tests, we can place the monetary policy convergence story on a much more solid empirical foundation. If we cannot find evidence of systematic monetary convergence, then we need to explore the origins of OECD monetary policy divergence after 1973.

CHAPTER 3

Evidence of Monetary Divergence

The first research question posed in chapter 1 asked if we can observe much evidence of widespread, or systematic, monetary policy convergence among the OECD countries in the post–Bretton Woods era. In response to this question, conventional wisdom answers in the affirmative: monetary policy convergence can be seen in the series of monetary and exchange rate regimes developed in Western Europe since the end of the Bretton Woods era in the early 1970s. Furthermore, many other governments not participating directly in these multilateral regimes made similar unilateral commitments to peg their national currencies, thus also committing them to the path of external monetary convergence for exchange rate stability.

However, as was discussed in chapter 2, we cannot judge external monetary convergence and the loss of domestic monetary autonomy simply by looking at whether or not a government has made a de jure commitment to stabilize its exchange rate, either unilaterally or within a multilateral currency arrangement, such as the European Snake or the European Monetary System. These exchange rate regimes were quite flexible arrangements allowing member states to maintain a surprisingly high degree of domestic policy autonomy if they so desired it. Thus, for every state achieving relative currency stability within the exchange rate mechanism (ERM) of the EMS, such as Belgium and the Netherlands, it is possible to identify another state asserting domestic policy autonomy with more variable exchange rates within the regime, such as France[1] or Italy.[2] Barnes (1996, 173) observed, "The ERM currencies often

1. France under Socialist Party governance is one of the two case studies in chapter 6.
2. Despite the wider bands granted to the government, Italy nonetheless realigned its currency within the EMS on a fairly regular basis. Gros and Thygesen (1992, 68) documented twelve multiple currency realignments inside this regime from 1979 through 1990, with Italy participating in nine (in September 1979, March 1981, October 1981, June 1982, March 1983, July 1985, April

appeared no more stable than other currencies, [and] the inflation rates were similar to those found world wide."[3]

In addition, for every state achieving relative exchange rate stability with a unilateral commitment to peg its currency, such as Austria, it is possible to identify another state with a very flexible unilateral peg, such as Sweden.[4] Finally, many states with no formal commitments to fix the value of their national currencies nonetheless achieved a significant degree of exchange rate stability: two examples are the United Kingdom,[5] especially in the late 1980s, and Japan.[6] Various economists have extensively documented the historical disconnect between governments' stated monetary commitments and the actual stability of national currency values (see, e.g., Reinhart and Rogoff 2004; Shambaugh 2004; Levy-Yeyati and Sturzenegger 2005). For scholars of international monetary politics, the observed gap between such monetary "words and deeds" (see Levy-Yeyati and Sturzenegger 2005) means that we cannot treat fixed exchange rate commitments in any form as simple proxies for external currency stability and the corresponding loss of domestic policy autonomy. We also cannot treat the lack of any formal monetary commitments as prima facie evidence of domestic policy autonomy with exchange rate volatility.

Thus, to move forward in determining whether there has been systematic monetary policy convergence among the advanced industrial democracies in the post–Bretton Woods era, we clearly need a better way to measure external

---

1986, January 1987, and January 1990). The cumulative currency adjustment during this period was greater for Italy than for any other EMS member state.

3. For additional evidence on this point, see Grilli, Masciandro, and Tabellini 1991; Froot and Rogoff 1991; Eichengreen 1992; Fratianni and von Hagen 1992; Woolley 1992.

4. The Swedish exchange rate peg was flexibly constructed, and Social Democratic governments devalued the krona for competitive reasons on a regular basis, especially in the early 1980s. As Bernanke et al. (1999, 176–77) concluded, the "changes over time in the definition of the [Swedish] exchange-rate target, in response to changing circumstances, illustrate how a degree of flexibility may be introduced even into supposedly inflexible monetary regimes." Aylott (2001, 161) and Moses (1998, 207) made very similar arguments about how the unilateral Sweden exchange rate peg disguised a high degree of Swedish monetary independence.

5. The United Kingdom under Conservative Party governance is the second case study in chapter 6.

6. As Henning (1994, 121) explained, "exchange rate policy has consistently been an element of overall economic strategy in Japan" despite the lack of external currency commitments. Cargill, Hutchison, and Ito (1997, 62) similarly concluded: "International factors, such as the exchange rate, the balance of payments, and efforts to coordinate policy internationally, have influenced the conduct and control of Bank of Japan policy. Even after the breakup of the Bretton Woods system, but especially after the Plaza Agreement of 1985, the Bank of Japan remained very much concerned with external factors in formulating monetary policy despite the lack of formally binding exchange-rate and balance of payment constraints."

monetary policy convergence under the condition of international capital mobility. This is all the more true since political scientists have been using the term *monetary policy autonomy* for over a decade without defining precisely what they mean. Much as was the case with Justice Stewart's infamous definition of obscenity—"I know it when I see it"—the lack of a precise operational definition precludes scholarly progress.

This chapter proceeds in three sequential steps. The first step is to present a precise operational measure for external monetary convergence, or the loss of domestic monetary autonomy; the operational definition is borrowed from the interest parity condition in open-economy macroeconomics. The second step is to validate the measure using a construct validity test provided by the Mundell-Fleming framework. Having demonstrated its validity, we can then proceed to the third, final, and most important step in this chapter: assessing the extent of external monetary policy convergence among the OECD economies after 1973.

While the evidence suggests an important international capital mobility constraint on national monetary policy in the post–Bretton Woods era, there is little evidence of external monetary convergence on any systematic basis. Thus, the fact that international capital mobility constrains national monetary policy choices does not mean that it has also produced systematic monetary convergence. While some OECD governments have moved toward greater external monetary convergence, many others retained a significant amount of domestic monetary autonomy, despite the costs associated with this choice. Consequently, the post–Bretton Woods era is better characterized by the concept of monetary policy divergence, defined as the situation where OECD governments have used their national monetary policy for different purposes, with some working for greater external currency stability while many others pursued domestic monetary autonomy.

I. Measuring External Monetary Convergence

To measure the extent of external monetary convergence and its converse, domestic monetary autonomy, I propose an operational indicator from the field of open-economy macroeconomics. Economists commonly express the monetary autonomy–exchange rate stability trade-off under full capital mobility in terms of an interest parity condition (see Rose 1994, 30).[7]

---

7. Rose (1994, 30) presented a continuous-time version of uncovered interest parity. Here I present the discrete-time equivalent.

$$\Delta e = i - i^* \tag{3.1}$$

Equation (3.1) is known as uncovered interest parity, where Δe is a measure of exchange rate movements, i represents the domestic interest rate, and i^* represents the prevailing external, or world, interest rate. This equation states that the expected change in the exchange rate e is given by a nominal interest rate differential, the domestic interest rate minus the external interest rate. If a government wants to keep its exchange rate stable ($\Delta e \rightarrow 0$), then it must move its domestic interest rate in line with the prevailing world interest rate ($i \rightarrow i^*$). This movement of domestic interest rates toward the world interest rate defines the process known as external monetary policy convergence. If the two interest rates are the same ($i = i^*$), then external monetary policy convergence is theoretically complete. Conversely, holding a national interest rate that differs significantly from the prevailing world interest rate can be defined as domestic monetary policy autonomy.

Political scientists seem comfortable with the idea that a negative interest rate differential ($i < i^*$) fits the definition of monetary policy autonomy. But it is important to understand that domestic policy autonomy is also consistent with a positive interest rate differential ($i > i^*$), a situation that may result from fiscal policy expansion. The relationship between national interest rates and government spending in the post–Bretton Woods era will be discussed in more detail in chapter 4. At this point, I simply state that fiscal policy looseness may produce inflationary expectations, leading governments to use their monetary policy instrument for inflation control—an internal policy goal consistent with domestic monetary autonomy [8]—rather than for the external goal of exchange rate stability. This story certainly fits the expected monetary convergence process in Western Europe, where prospective EMU member states were required to reduce their fiscal deficits and public debt and to lower nominal interest rates in order to converge on the low-inflation states in the European Union (see Watson 1997).

Some political scientists may be surprised to discover that macroeconomists measure domestic monetary autonomy by a country's nominal interest rate differential, not by its real interest rate differential. This is true not because national inflation rates are unimportant but because the nominal interest rate

---

8. Recall the definition of monetary policy autonomy given in chapter 2: the ability of national governments to direct monetary policy instruments toward domestic economic objectives, including national economic growth and domestic price stability. This is why economists identify an inflation-targeting monetary policy as consistent with domestic monetary autonomy (see Bernanke et al. 1999).

differential fully reflects any expected inflation differential when capital is fully mobile. To understand this logic, it is useful to rewrite the right-hand side of the interest parity condition in terms of real interest rates (r) and expected inflation rates (π): $(i - i^*) = (r + \pi) - (r^* + \pi^*)$. With full capital mobility, the real interest rate differential is assumed to be zero; hence, $r - r^* = 0$. If the real interest rate differential is not zero, capital can be expected to move until such differential real returns are equalized. With full capital mobility, the r terms effectively cancel and the nominal interest rate differential fully reflects any differential rates of expected inflation: $(i - i^*) = (\pi - \pi^*)$.[9] On this point, it is important to note that inflationary expectations often differ from actual inflation rates. Due to different policy choices made by governments, national economies may have very different inflationary expectations even when their actual inflation rates do not differ significantly.

As this logic also illustrates, real interest rate differentials signify the extent to which money can move across national borders to equalize real returns. Thus, real interest rate differentials, much like covered interest rate differentials, do not capture the concept of domestic monetary policy autonomy as it is understood in open-economy macroeconomics.[10] Instead, these interest rate differentials measure the extent of international capital mobility—an entirely different menu item in the Mundell-Fleming framework (see Frankel 1991; Shepherd 1994).[11]

Given international capital mobility, the uncovered interest parity condition offers a very tractable way to measure domestic monetary autonomy versus external monetary convergence. Using this simple measure, domestic monetary autonomy (or external monetary convergence) can be defined as the extent to which a country's nominal interest rate differs from (or approaches) the prevailing external, or world, interest rate. As face validity for this approach to measuring domestic monetary autonomy versus external monetary conver-

9. This is consistent with Moses's simple definition (1998, 214) of domestic monetary autonomy as excess inflation or, more correctly, positive inflationary expectations.

10. This is why Garrett and Lange's data (1991, 551–52) on real interest rates and real growth in money supply do not indicate monetary policy convergence. Instead, their data simply capture the fact of international capital mobility among this set of OECD economies. This is worth mentioning because their data are still sometimes cited in the literature as evidence of systematic monetary policy convergence among the OECD economies.

11. In addition to being measured by real interest rate differentials, international capital mobility has also been measured in terms of cross-border capital flows, national savings-investment coefficients, and the elimination of government restrictions on capital movements. Especially with the availability of Quinn and Inclan's (1997) data on OECD financial market openness, political scientists have tended to use the latter as the preferred measure of international capital mobility. I will do the same in the statistical models in this book.

gence, it is worth noting that Shambaugh (2004, 305–12) similarly used the interest parity condition as the basis for his examination of how national monetary policy is affected by de facto fixed exchange rates.

One possible objection to using the right-hand side of the uncovered interest parity condition as an operational indicator for domestic monetary autonomy and external monetary convergence is that it poorly predicts the direction of exchange rate movements.[12] In practice, positive interest rate differentials ($i > i^*$) are not always associated with currency appreciation. Often, a rise in national interest rates leads to currency depreciation. This directional ambiguity appears related to how international investors, with differing risk profiles, interpret a rise in national interest rates (see Willett, Khan, and Der Hovanessian 1985). If interpreted as a signal of higher returns on investments in the domestic market, it should lead to a currency appreciation. If viewed instead as a sign of increasing domestic inflationary expectations, then a rise in national interest rates may produce a depreciated currency.

This directional ambiguity does not mean that with international capital mobility, there is no trade-off between monetary policy autonomy and exchange rate stability. But it does suggest the need to consider an alternative measure of exchange rate instability, one that captures currency movements in both directions. Thus, I choose to measure national exchange rate variability in terms of a coefficient of variation (Ve), replacing the Δe term on the right-hand side of equation (3.1). The coefficient of variation captures the relative variability of the national currency measured against some external benchmark but makes no distinction with regard to the direction of exchange rate movements.[13]

At this point, it is important to state that I cannot and will not make any arguments about the direction of exchange rate movements or even about exchange rate levels in the post–Bretton Woods era. To do so would clearly require a different monetary model, and I leave this task to other scholars. That being said, the use of a directionless measure of national currency variability has now become a standard way to capture exchange rate instability (see, e.g., Rose 1994; Frieden 2002; Levy-Yeyati and Sturzenegger 2003, 2005). The big-

12. On this point, see Fama 1984; Frankel and Froot 1989.

13. The coefficient of variation (Ve) is calculated by dividing the standard deviation of exchange rate levels over a particular period (σe) by the mean value over the same period. In the pooled time-series models in this book, it would be incorrect to use the simple standard deviation statistic, which is an absolute measure of variability and, thus, is affected by the unit of measurement (i.e., the national currency unit), since the unit of measurement differs for each country in the sample.

ger question concerns the choice of an appropriate external benchmark against which to measure annual OECD national currency variability.

Scholars often use a single currency benchmark; for example, Frieden (2002) measured national currency variability versus the German mark. While this might be appropriate for the narrow sample of countries around Germany,[14] variability versus the German mark is clearly an unsuitable measure for the larger OECD sample including many countries in North America and the Pacific. Indeed, one of the major critiques of the systematic monetary convergence hypothesis was that its few empirical investigations tended to focus almost exclusively on its most favorable cross-sectional domain: countries in Western Europe or, even more narrowly, those within the European Union. If systematic monetary convergence is occurring in the post–Bretton Woods era—whether due to international capital mobility, neoliberal policy ideas, or interest group pressures—then the hypothesis must be tested on a much broader cross-sectional sample, which requires a different external currency benchmark.

Another possible single currency benchmark would be the U.S. dollar, as employed by Rose (1994), following the logic that the American currency has served more as a global currency than has the German mark. But a U.S. dollar benchmark would be potentially problematic for the sizable number of EU member states who have focused more on exchange rate stability versus the German currency than the U.S. dollar, at least since the late 1970s. Thus, we clearly need to measure national exchange rate variability relative to a broad basket of external currencies.

One obvious possibility would be to create a trade-weighted and capital-weighted measure of national currency variability. In practice, however, such a measure is problematic to construct for at least two reasons. First, the data on

14. It is arguably not even appropriate for this narrow sample. Given a theoretical story beginning with the preferences of diversified economic actors (exporters and investors) and their propensity to pressure governments when exchange rates become excessively unstable, any measure of exchange rate variability using a single currency benchmark, including the German mark, could be invalid. The potential validity problem can be illustrated with a series of examples: less than one-sixth of British exports, less than one-fifth of French and Italian exports, less than one-fourth of Belgian exports, and less than one-third of Dutch exports went to Germany in 1992, even though Germany is the largest trading partner of each of the corresponding states. Thus, even when using an all-European sample of countries, measuring currency variability relative to only the German mark might seriously misrepresent how much exchange rate instability is actually experienced by diversified traders and investors. Given a broader OECD sample, the validity problem would grow. At least in theory, when these economic actors encounter undesirable currency movements in one market, they can shift their business activities to other markets as an alternative to costly lobbying for exchange rate stability.

bilateral capital flows are extremely poor even for the advanced industrial democracies. Second and more important, if currency variability is supposed to determine trade levels (a common argument in the monetary convergence literature for why actors prefer fixed and stable exchange rates), then any trade-weighted measure of currency variability suffers from a serious endogeneity problem: trade levels are used to create the measure of currency variability, yet trade levels are also a function of currency stability.

To avoid this endogeneity problem and yet obtain an appropriately broad external benchmark, I choose to measure national currency variability relative to the Special Drawing Right (SDR), the International Monetary Fund's reserve currency based on a weighted average of the national currencies of the G-5, or Group of Five, which includes France, Germany, Japan, the United Kingdom, and the United States. This benchmark is also useful because it presents no extraordinary data demands, as national currency variability versus the SDR is regularly reported by the International Monetary Fund (IMF) in its *International Financial Statistics*. Inasmuch as the IMF basket currency reflects the value of three European currencies, including the German mark, French franc, and British pound, it serves as a suitable benchmark for all the European countries in the broad OECD sample used in the present study. Inasmuch as it also reflects the U.S. dollar and Japanese yen, it also serves as a suitable benchmark for the other North American and Pacific states included in the OECD sample. Finally, since each of the individual G-5 currencies experience variability versus the broader SDR benchmark, it is not necessary to exclude any G-5 government from my statistical analyses in this and the other chapters. This allows testing of the various arguments by using the full sample of OECD countries in the post–Bretton Woods era, although it will be necessary to include country-specific fixed effects in the statistical models of exchange rate variability.

Using this weighted G-5 benchmark, I calculated the variable EXRCV to indicate yearly national currency variability for twenty-three OECD countries from 1973 to 1997.[15] I began with 1973 because it marks the start of the post–Bretton Woods era. I stopped with 1997 because it is the year in which a large group of European countries in the OECD sample were expected to be policy convergent in preparation for the final stage of the EMU.

Figure 4 plots the time-series descriptive data for this operational measure of exchange rate variability, or instability. The graph suggests some obvious

15. The exchange rate data come from the International Monetary Fund's *International Financial Statistics*. I obtained a yearly coefficient of variation using monthly exchange rate values, the least temporally aggregated value available from this source.

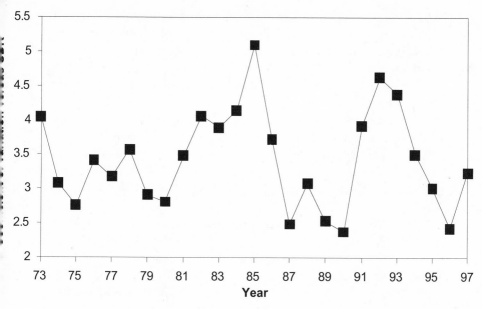

Fig. 4. Average OECD Exchange Rate Variability, 1973–97. (Exchange rate data
from International Monetary Fund, *International Financial Statistics.*)

face validity, as it shows a variability spike in 1984–85 (the exchange rate instability leading to the Plaza Accord), a period of relative currency stability from
1987 to 1990 (the era of the Louvre target zone), and a final spike corresponding to the 1992 exchange rate crisis in Western Europe. These time-series
descriptive data show no clear trend toward greater exchange rate stability, or
less currency variability, for the OECD states in the post–Bretton Woods era.
This interesting fact runs contrary to the theoretical expectations of the systematic monetary convergence hypothesis, which predicted that OECD governments would move toward exchange rate stability with greater international
capital mobility after 1973 (see fig. 3 in chap. 2).

2. Validating the Operational Measures

The nominal interest rate differential measure for domestic monetary autonomy and the indicator of exchange rate variability detailed in the preceding
section can and should be subjected to stronger validity tests than simple face

validity.[16] One very important and straightforward construct validity test comes directly from the Mundell-Fleming framework. In the post–Bretton Woods era of international capital mobility, greater domestic monetary policy autonomy should be associated with more exchange rate variability. Thus, valid operational measures for these two theoretical concepts must exhibit a strong positive relationship.

To estimate this relationship, I begin with the simple statistical model described in equation (3.2), using the sample of OECD countries over the 1973–97 period, with country-year specified as the unit of analysis.[17]

$$EXRCV_{it} = \beta_0 + \beta_1 {}^*MONAUT_{it} + \alpha_i {}^*COUNTRY_i + \alpha_t {}^*YEAR_t + e_{it} \qquad (3.2)$$

The dependent variable, EXRCV, indicates the coefficient of nominal variation for the country's currency versus the SDR in year t. The main independent variable is MONAUT (monetary autonomy), measuring the country-year nominal interest rate differential in absolute terms ($|i - i^*|$), since domestic interest rates either below or above the prevailing external interest rate would indicate a more independent monetary policy stance. To capture most accurately the policy choice made by national monetary authorities, i is the country's policy interest rate, rather than a market interest rate.[18] The prevailing external interest rate, or world interest rate (i^*,) is calculated as the weighted (by gross domestic product) average of the G-5 countries' policy interest rates, since these countries are the world's largest capital-producing economies and, thus, effectively set the world interest rate.[19]

To control for country risk and exogenous shocks that may impact national exchange rate variability, I follow Rose (1994) in adding dummy variables for all countries in the sample except the United States and for all years except

16. On different approaches to validation, see Manheim, Rich, and Willnat 2002, 69–73.

17. There are twenty-three OECD countries in the sample, and each country was measured over twenty-five years. Thus, there are 575 country-year observations. The OECD sample consists of the following countries in alphabetical order: Australia, Austria, Belgium, Canada, Denmark, Finland, France, Germany, Greece, Ireland, Italy, Japan, Luxembourg, the Netherlands, New Zealand, Norway, Portugal, Spain, Sweden, Switzerland, Turkey, the United Kingdom, and the United States.

18. As the main policy interest rate, I use the federal funds rate equivalent from the International Monetary Fund's *International Financial Statistics,* line 60b, as recommended by Reinhart and Rogoff (2004, 27). When this series is missing, I use line 60c, as done in Calvo and Reinhart's 2002 study.

19. For each G-5 state in the sample, I make an important adjustment. The interest rate differential for the United States, Japan, Germany, Britain, and France is measured relative to the other G-5 states.

1973. As the errors in this time-series cross-sectional model are likely to exhibit contemporaneous autocorrelation and panel heteroskedasticity, I estimate the model using panel-corrected standard errors (PCSEs). To correct for serial autocorrelation in each country time series, I also estimate and adjust for first-order autocorrelation.[20] The results thus provide Prais-Winsten generalized least squares, rather than ordinary least squares, coefficients.

The Mundell-Fleming construct validity test requires that the MONAUT coefficient be positively signed and statistically significant. In other words, larger absolute interest rate differentials, or greater domestic monetary autonomy, should have produced more exchange rate variability in the post–Bretton Woods era, although the result cannot speak to the direction of exchange rate movements after 1973. The estimates, shown in the first column of table 2, confirm this expectation, demonstrating some important construct validity for the measures of domestic monetary autonomy and exchange rate stability that will be used here and in later chapters.

In the second column of table 2, I reestimated the equation, adding a control variable for international capital mobility. Following Clark and Reichert (1998), equation (3.2) originally assumed that capital was internationally mobile at the end of the Bretton Woods system and, thus, could be treated as a given in the post–Bretton Woods era, at least for the OECD economies. But it may be useful to control for variation with regard to capital openness after 1973.[21] Extending the data from Quinn and Inclan (1997), KOPEN (capital openness) measures country i's financial openness in year t on a 0–14 scale, with larger values indicating more open national capital markets. The time-series descriptive data for Quinn and Inclan's measure are shown in figure 5.

20. Recent papers (e.g., Achen 2000; Kristensen and Wawro 2003) have begun to question the use of a lagged dependent variable, especially with PCSEs, as originally recommended by Beck and Katz (1995). Among other potential problems, a lagged dependent variable tends to bias other coefficients in the model toward zero. Since I will draw substantive conclusions from the statistically significant and insignificant variables, it becomes important to simultaneously minimize both Type I and Type II errors. Not correcting for serial autocorrelation tends to produce overconfident standard errors, leading to Type I errors. But the attenuation bias associated with the lagged dependent variable risks Type II errors. Keele and Kelly (2004) have shown that this bias becomes smaller with longer time series but that the bias can be quite severe with only twenty-five observation time series (as pooled here). I thus choose the AR1 (first order autoregression) correction for serial autocorrelation. Lagrange multiplier tests on the residuals after the AR1 correction reveal no statistically significant evidence of first-order serial autocorrelation.

21. As Andrews (1994b, 195) correctly noted, international capital mobility is best defined not in terms of actual capital flows but in terms of the capacity of money to move across international borders. Indeed, once real interest rates have completely converged, there may be little reason for capital to move even though it is fully able to do so.

Their data reveal that the average OECD country was already quite open in financial terms at the beginning of the post–Bretton Woods era. This is an important point to which I will return later.

With this new variable added to the model, it is important to note the prediction made by the first-wave monetary convergence hypothesis, which argued that growing international capital mobility led governments toward external monetary convergence to achieve greater exchange rate stability (see fig. 3 in chap. 2). If this monetary convergence logic is correct, the KOPEN coefficient should be statistically significant and negatively signed, indicating less national currency variability. The results in the second column of table 2 tend to disconfirm this hypothesis, as KOPEN has a weak positive coefficient. It is also interesting to note that the estimated coefficient for the MONAUT variable scarcely changes with the addition of the KOPEN control variable, demonstrating once again the strong positive relationship between domestic monetary autonomy and exchange rate variability in the post–Bretton Woods era.

TABLE 2. Estimates of the Trade-off between Monetary Autonomy and Exchange Rate Variability

	1	2	3	4	5
Constant	3.07***	2.58**	3.27***	3.27***	−0.48
	(0.35)	(1.09)	(1.18)	(1.17)	(1.28)
MONAUT	0.19***	0.18***	0.07	0.07	
	(0.04)	(0.04)	(0.13)	(0.13)	
KOPEN		0.04	−0.02	−0.02	0.29***
		(0.09)	(0.10)	(0.10)	(0.11)
MONAUT × KOPEN			0.01	0.01	
			(0.01)	(0.01)	
EMS				−0.21	−0.23
				(0.36)	(0.38)
SNAKE				−0.40	0.09
				(0.49)	(0.49)
UNIPEG				−0.08	0.25
				(0.34)	(0.38)
X^2 for country fixed effects	2709.05***	806.65***	277.97***	246.91***	489.33***
X^2 for year fixed effects	1439.35***	1303.65***	1375.65***	1468.25***	1070.98***
N	575	575	575	575	575
R^2	0.55	0.55	0.57	0.57	0.35

Note: Estimates are Prais-Winsten coefficients, including an AR1 correction, with panel-corrected standard errors in parentheses. Individual country and year dummies are not reported.

Two-tailed statistical significance is indicated as follows: ***$p < .01$, **$p < .05$, *$p < .10$.

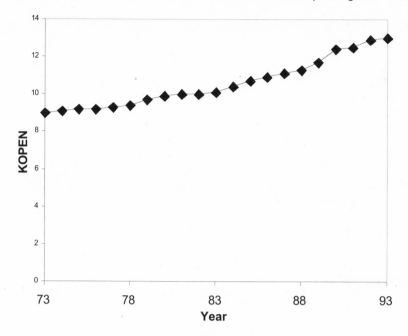

Fig. 5.   Average OECD Financial Openness, 1973–93.
(Data from Quinn and Inclan 1997.)

Next, I added the interaction term MONAUT*KOPEN to assess whether the trade-off between domestic monetary autonomy and exchange rate stability has strengthened with growing international capital mobility in the post–Bretton Woods era. With the interaction term, the marginal effect of MONAUT now depends on two different coefficients and the value of KOPEN: β_1*MONAUT + β_2*MONAUT*KOPEN. When KOPEN = 0 (a completely closed national capital market), the marginal effect of a one-unit increase in MONAUT is simply $\beta1$. When KOPEN = 14 (a completely open national capital market), the marginal effect of a one-unit increase in MONAUT becomes $\beta1 + \beta2*14$. Figure 6 plots the changing marginal effect of MONAUT given the different possible values for KOPEN, using the results from the third column of table 2.

As anticipated by the Mundell-Fleming framework, figure 6 shows that the trade-off between monetary autonomy and exchange rate stability has indeed grown with increasing international capital mobility. At low levels of KOPEN (0–5), the marginal effect of domestic monetary autonomy on external currency variability was not statistically different from zero with greater than 95

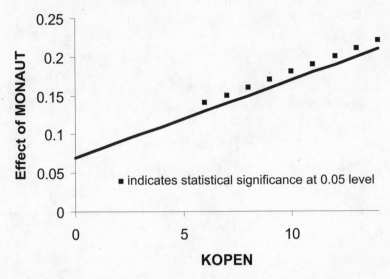

Fig. 6.   The Marginal Effect of Monetary Autonomy (MONAUT)
on Exchange Rate Variability (EXRCV)

percent confidence. But when KOPEN $\geq$ 6, monetary independence has a strong substantive and statistical effect on exchange rate variability. Looking back at figure 5, the average OECD economy began the post–Bretton Woods era with a KOPEN value of 9. Thus, the trade-off between domestic monetary autonomy and exchange rate stability has been quite strong throughout the period under study, and it appears reasonable to treat the international capital mobility constraint largely as a given after 1973, at least for the OECD countries.

Because I argued earlier that de jure commitments (either unilateral or multilateral) to fix the value of the national currency should not be treated as a strong proxy for actual exchange rate stability, it becomes useful to provide some additional evidence on this point. In the fourth column of table 2, I added three dummy variables for different OECD exchange rate commitments in the post–Bretton Woods era. EMS is coded as 1 if country i was a member of the exchange rate mechanism of the EMS in year t; otherwise, it is coded as 0. SNAKE is coded as 1 if country i was a member of the European Snake in year t; otherwise, it is coded as 0. Finally, UNIPEG is coded as 1 if country i made a unilateral declaration to peg its currency for year t; otherwise, it is coded as 0. If these de jure commitments have really produced a more stable national currency, their coefficients should be negatively signed and statistically significant.

The results show that while each of the new variables take on the expected negative coefficient, all three fall well short of statistical significance. It is perhaps not surprising that SNAKE and UNIPEG were not associated with strong reductions in national currency variability, given the well-documented weakness of the European Snake regime[22] and the inherent flexibility associated with unilateral decisions to peg the national currency. But the statistically weak EMS result may surprise some readers. It is certainly possible that the EMS coefficient was pushed toward zero due to collinearity with the MONAUT terms, following the logic that EMS membership reduced domestic monetary independence and, thus, that any EMS effect would be diluted in the presence of the monetary autonomy indicator. To explore this possibility, I dropped MONAUT and its interaction term in the fifth column of table 2. But even in this more restricted model, the estimated EMS effect in reducing national currency variability remains weak, a result that is consistent with Marston's conclusion (1995, 135) that the EMS "has fallen somewhat short of its objectives" and "not managed to stabilize [the] exchange rates" of member states.

In response to this evidence, one might argue, with good reason, that the EMS result would have been stronger had I focused more narrowly on national exchange rate variability versus the German mark, effectively the EMS anchor currency.[23] But it is important to remember that the German mark's value is reflected in the SDR benchmark, as is the French franc, the second largest EMS currency. As some economists have argued, "the decisive criterion" for judging exchange rate stability should be "whether the EMS has reduced the variability of the *global average,* or effective, exchange rates of the currencies participating in the ERM" (Gros and Thygesen 1992, 105; emphasis added). The results presented here, much like those offered earlier by Vaubel (1989), demonstrate that when using an appropriately broad measure of exchange rate stability, it becomes much harder to find any strong EMS effects.

To summarize briefly before proceeding to look at the extent of domestic monetary autonomy after 1973, this empirical exercise has illustrated two important points. First, the operational measures that will be used to capture both monetary policy autonomy and exchange rate instability have the essential property that is expected by the Mundell-Fleming framework: larger absolute interest rate differentials are associated with greater national currency variability when controlling for and interacted with international capital mobility. This demonstration shows how these operational measures pass a

22. On this point, see Gros and Thygesen 1992; Ungerer 1997; McNamara 1998.
23. Indeed, Frieden (2002, 853) and I (Bearce 2003, 406) reported that membership in the European Snake and the EMS was significantly associated with less currency variability relative to the German mark.

very important construct validity test. Second, the empirical results also show that we cannot capture exchange rate stability and related monetary policy choices simply by looking at whether or not a government has made a political commitment to fix the value of its national currency. It may well be the case that OECD governments, especially those in Western Europe, are increasingly making such commitments, but this fact cannot be treated as strong evidence of either greater exchange rate stability or the corresponding loss of domestic policy autonomy.

3. Monetary Policy Divergence after 1973

Having presented operational measures for both domestic monetary autonomy and exchange rate variability (the first step of the study in this chapter) and having then demonstrated their validity using a test from the Mundell-Fleming framework (the second step), we can now assess the extent of external monetary policy convergence (or divergence) for the OECD countries in the post–Bretton Woods era (the crucial third step). The time-series descriptive data for one of the two external monetary policy convergence indicators—exchange rate stability—was presented in figure 4. These data showed no real trend toward greater exchange rate stability, or reduced currency variability, for OECD governments after 1973, a finding that runs contrary to the theoretical expectations of the monetary convergence hypothesis. Similar descriptive data for the other operational indicator—domestic monetary autonomy as measured by the average nominal interest rate differential—can be presented to assess the trend (or lack thereof) toward external monetary convergence, or smaller interest rate differentials, after 1973.

But before looking at these data, it is useful to think carefully about how a pattern of monetary policy convergence would present itself. Inasmuch as the OECD countries are thought to have held substantial domestic monetary autonomy at the beginning of the post–Bretton Woods era and then to have increasingly lost it after 1973 (see figs. 2–3 in chap. 2), the systematic monetary policy convergence hypothesis suggests that the average OECD nominal interest rate differential should show a strong trend toward zero over time, as illustrated in figure 7. If there is only a weak trend toward zero, this might be consistent with episodic, but not necessarily systematic, monetary policy convergence. To the extent that average OECD nominal interest differential is growing for part or all of the post–Bretton Woods era, the dominant trend would be toward greater domestic monetary autonomy, despite its apparent costs with international capital mobility.

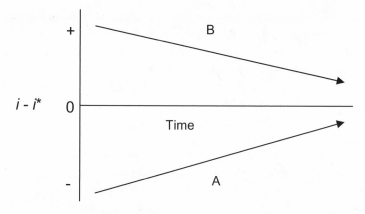

Fig. 7.   The Hypothesized Trend toward Systematic Monetary Policy Convergence

Figure 7 shows two different trend lines consistent with the monetary policy convergence hypothesis. The first possibility is that OECD governments asserted domestic monetary autonomy during the Bretton Woods system in the form of negative interest rate differentials ($i < i^*$) and then raised national interest rates after 1973 to minimize their interest rate differential, as illustrated by path A. It is important to note that external monetary convergence would also be consistent with the trend illustrated by path B, where OECD governments formerly held positive interest rate differentials ($i > i^*$) and then reduced national interest rates toward the low prevailing external interest rate.

I can find no statement in the monetary convergence literature describing the direction in which national interest rates are expected to move in order to achieve external monetary policy convergence. Instead, systematic monetary convergence has been expressed in terms of economic outcomes, such as stable exchange rates and low inflation, as discussed in chapter 2. This suggests an important lack of theoretical development, at least in terms of what these economic outcomes mean for national interest rates. For example, should national interest rates be rising to counter inflationary expectations, or should they be falling consistent with the achievement of lower inflation? Similarly, should national interest rates rise or fall to achieve greater exchange rate stability? Thus far, the political science scholarship on monetary policy convergence has not addressed these important questions. But to be generous, it should be possible to accept the hypothesis of systematic monetary policy convergence if the data fall along either path A or path B.

To be even more generous to the hypothesis of systematic monetary policy convergence, the data in figure 8 show the average OECD nominal interest rate differential over time after excluding the country with the largest interest rate differential in each year.[24] This exclusion has the effect of pushing the average OECD interest rate differential toward zero, potentially biasing the results in favor of systematic monetary policy convergence. But since I cannot control for the different factors that may affect the variation in OECD national interest rates with simple descriptive statistics, this exclusion helps avoid the situation of an outlier country exerting undue influence on the OECD sample.[25] Despite this favorable setup, figure 8 clearly shows that the average OECD nominal interest rate differential corresponds to neither of the two possible paths toward systematic monetary policy convergence for most of the post–Bretton Woods era.

After looking at these data, three important points should be noted and discussed. First, these data suggest that OECD governments, on average, began the post–Bretton Woods era with a relatively convergent monetary policy stance (nominal interest rate differentials close to zero), revealing the loss of domestic monetary autonomy at the end of the Bretton Woods system. While perhaps surprising to scholars who have viewed the Bretton Woods system as one where national governments held substantial domestic monetary independence, this finding is quite consistent with data presented by Quinn and Inclan (1997), showing that most OECD governments had opened their national capital markets well before the end of the Bretton Woods system (on this point, see also fig. 5). Thus, in its final years, the Bretton Woods system became marked by a surprisingly high degree of international capital mobility. This fact, coupled with the Bretton Woods fixed exchange rate regime, made domestic monetary autonomy somewhat difficult to achieve before the system ended in the early 1970s (see Gowa 1983).[26]

24. For most years, this country is Turkey, the lowest income OECD member state.

25. In the statistical models where OECD national interest rates are the dependent variable, I control for these factors by including gross domestic product per capita and country-specific fixed effects as independent variables. Thus, I model the important differences among this set of countries, rather than excluding particular OECD member states.

26. Indeed, the loss of domestic monetary autonomy toward the end of the Bretton Woods system helps explain why many OECD governments acquiesced in ending the system's fixed exchange rate regime. They could not forestall growing international capital mobility, and they wanted to regain the domestic policy independence that had been effectively lost in the late 1960s and early 1970s. As Webb (1991, 311) wrote, the "fixed exchange rate system was abandoned in the early 1970s, when increasing capital mobility made it impossible for governments to stabilize exchange rates without subordinating monetary policy to that end."

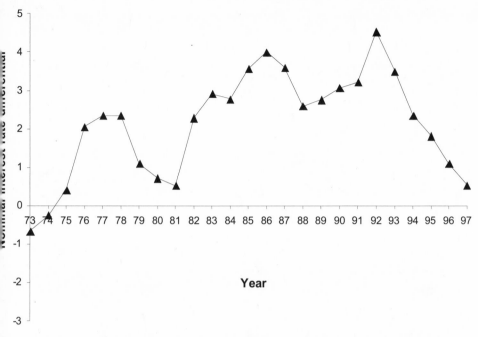

Fig. 8.   Average OECD Nominal Interest Rate Differential, 1973–97. (Monetary policy data from International Monetary Fund, *International Financial Statistics*.)

Second, and more important for the systematic monetary convergence hypothesis, the data show no strong trend toward external monetary convergence, or smaller interest rate differentials, over this twenty-five-year period, except after 1994. As was discussed in chapter 2, it is not particularly hard to explain how external monetary convergence was possible in the late 1990s, since much of the global North experienced a brief period of noninflationary growth, where societal demands for domestic policy independence effectively lessened—even disappeared (see Gobbin and Van Aarle 2001; Von Hagen and Strauch 2001). That there is not even a weak trend toward smaller nominal interest rate differentials in figure 8 for most of the post–Bretton Woods era is consistent with the hypothesis of OECD monetary policy divergence after 1973.

Additional support for OECD monetary policy divergence after 1973 can be seen in figure 9, which plots the variation around the yearly interest rate differential average using a standard deviation measure of variability. If the advanced industrial democracies were really converging on any particular interest rate

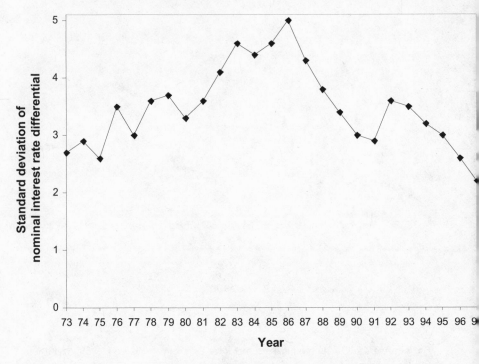

Fig. 9.   Variation in OECD Monetary Autonomy, 1973–97

differential outcome (either positive or negative), we should expect to see a strong trend of declining variability over time. At the very most, there is only a very weak trend, limited to the 1990s.[27] Even during the 1990s, the variation measure remains well above zero, suggesting OECD monetary policy divergence even during a period when external monetary policy convergence was relatively easy to achieve.

Third, and most important for the analysis to come in chapter 4, the data shown in figure 8 evidences that domestic monetary policy autonomy in the post–Bretton Woods era has been largely characterized by national interest rates that are higher on a nominal basis than the world interest rate. This fact

27. If I include all OECD member states without dropping the country with the largest interest rate differential, there is actually a slight trend toward greater variation over time. This finding accords with Froot and Rogoff's conclusion (1991, 271) that "the degree of monetary-policy convergence is generally overstated" even for Western Europe, the most favorable region for the monetary convergence hypothesis.

suggests an important international capital mobility constraint on domestic policy choices. If national governments engage in behavior that is viewed as potentially inflationary by international investors, they will have to raise national interest rates for greater domestic price stability. But this international capital mobility constraint has certainly not led to any systematic monetary policy convergence. Just the opposite appears to be the case; many OECD governments have been willing to accept domestic monetary independence in the form of positive nominal interest rate differentials.

This fact may strike some readers as surprising, especially those who have conceived of domestic monetary policy autonomy exclusively in terms of holding negative nominal interest rate differentials. Indeed, if we look at monetary policy in complete isolation, then domestic monetary independence in the form of positive interest rate differentials would be quite perplexing. But as I argued in chapters 1 and 2, divorcing monetary policy choices from those of fiscal policy is a mistake. We should instead consider how governments might coordinate their fiscal and monetary policy instruments in an effort to achieve multiple economic policy goals given the constraints imposed by international capital mobility in the post–Bretton Woods era. It may be the case that when governments engage in fiscal expansion to promote economic growth, they must also raise interest rates for domestic price stability. In this sense, domestic monetary independence would be directly related to fiscal policy expansion and autonomy. Indeed, when placed in this broader policy mix context, domestic monetary autonomy in the form of positive national interest rate differentials becomes more comprehensible. This is the important subject to which chapter 4 is devoted.

But before proceeding to chapter 4, with its explanation for domestic monetary policy autonomy in the form of positive nominal interest rate differentials, it is useful to conclude this chapter with a brief consideration of why the "world" interest rate—as defined by the weighted average of the G-5 economies—has been and can be expected to remain relatively low, at least on a nominal basis. First, consider the fact that most of the world's capital has been created within these five largest and most developed capitalist economies and that there is a distinct home bias with regard to investment decisions (see Schulze and Ursprung 1999, 345). Consequently, even with international capital mobility, much of the world's capital remained concentrated in these national economies, making the local supply of money more generous relative to the demand. Hence, it is not surprising to observe a lower nominal interest rate, reflecting the cheaper price of capital, in the more developed national economies.

Second, it is important to consider, as was discussed earlier, that nominal interest rates are also an indicator of national inflation rates and inflationary expectations. To the extent that larger and more developed capitalist economies are likely to have more producers competing on the basis of price considerations, it may be easier for them to keep prices stable and, therefore, to keep nominal interest rates low.[28] Together, these considerations help explain why the so-called world interest rate in the post–Bretton Woods era has been relatively low on a nominal basis. Consequently, external monetary convergence required most OECD governments to achieve the domestic economic conditions that would allow them to lower national interest rates. Certainly, this should have been easier for more developed capitalist economies for the two reasons already mentioned. Thus, when we model national interest rates and related domestic policy choices, it will be important to control for variation in economic development among the different OECD economies across time and space.

But this is not the only factor explaining national interest rates, and for political scientists, it may not even be the most interesting one. Chapter 4 will enrich the story by considering how the fiscal policy decisions made by OECD governments affect national interest rates and how these governments effectively coordinate their fiscal and monetary policy instruments to achieve both economic growth and lower inflation given the external constraints imposed by international capital mobility. In doing so, it will provide a broader context for understanding macroeconomic policy divergence in the post–Bretton Woods era.

---

28. On this point, my data set shows a statistically significant negative correlation for both gross domestic product and gross domestic product per capita with inflation.

CHAPTER 4

From Fiscal to Monetary Divergence

Chapter 3 established that little evidence exists to support the hypothesis of systematic monetary policy convergence among the advanced industrial democracies in the post–Bretton Woods era. Many OECD governments have opted for domestic monetary autonomy in the form of positive nominal interest rate differentials. The evidence showing a lack of external monetary policy convergence, or smaller interest rate differentials, is consistent with the data showing no trend toward greater exchange rate stability, or reduced currency variability, for the OECD governments after 1973. Thus, the post–Bretton Woods era is better characterized by the description of monetary policy divergence with international capital mobility.

Chapter 3 also ended with a puzzle: why have many advanced industrial democracies asserted domestic monetary autonomy in the form of positive nominal interest rate differentials? Put somewhat differently, why have many OECD governments chosen national interest rates that are higher on a nominal basis than the low external interest rate?[1] To help resolve this apparent puzzle, I propose that we think more about the linkages between national monetary and fiscal policy choices, theorizing about why and how the advanced industrial democracies may have used their different policy instruments to meet multiple economic policy goals in an era of international capital mobility.

As some scholars have noted (see, e.g., Way 2000), the political science discipline has not engaged in much theoretical work concerning how governments choose their fiscal and monetary policy mix. Instead, there has been a long-standing tendency to focus more on policy goals and outcomes (e.g., economic growth or inflation) while ignoring the important question of which

---

1. For further evidence showing that the external interest rate is low on a nominal basis, see Shambaugh 2004, 321.

policy instruments were used to achieve such objectives (see, e.g., Hibbs 1977; Alt 1985). Webb (1994, 400) has argued: "Expansion or restraint could be achieved by a variety of means, and analysts [need to] pay attention to the mix between monetary and fiscal policy instruments. Different policy mixes may have similar macroeconomic effects but different distributional effects and international effects." These effects include those related to exchange rate stability.

Some recent work (see, e.g., Oatley 1999; Clark and Hallerberg 2000; Clark 2003) has done a much better job in focusing on the use of policy instruments, examining how governments condition their fiscal and monetary policy choices on their exchange rate regime (assumed to be either fixed or floating). This work is also a major advance because it does not build from the assumption of monetary policy convergence; thus, it departs from the third wave of political science research on this topic (see table 1 in chap. 1). Indeed, scholars have arguably launched a fourth wave of political science research on this topic, explicitly exploring the nature of monetary policy divergence with international capital mobility. But this line of research does have certain limitations, in that it treats the government's exchange rate regime as exogenously determined and focuses primarily on de jure exchange rate regimes.

I thus propose a different line of research, one that focuses more directly on de facto exchange rate regimes, or actual exchange rate stability. Furthermore, this new line of research treats exchange rate stability as an endogenous policy outcome with regard to the government's monetary and fiscal policy choices. Exchange rates are not fixed simply because a government declares them to be so. They become fixed—or at least more stable—when and if a government makes internal policy decisions consistent with external currency stability. If a government instead asserts domestic policy autonomy, which I will show to include certain fiscal policy choices, then exchange rates will become more variable, or unstable, with international capital mobility, despite any de jure commitments otherwise.

This chapter proceeds in four parts. The first part establishes some microfoundations in discussing why governments must work toward two dominant economic policy goals—economic growth and low inflation—given international capital mobility. The important point is that governments cannot focus all their efforts on only one of these goals while ignoring the other. This fact effectively forces governments to move their fiscal and monetary policy instruments in opposite directions in an effort to achieve concurrently these two different—and often difficult to reconcile—economic objectives.

Using this logic, the second part hypothesizes that OECD governments have moved onto a particular policy mix continuum in the post–Bretton Woods era. This policy mix continuum is defined by high government spending with high nominal interest rates on one end and low government spending with low nominal interest rates on the other end. Another policy mix continuum, where government spending moves in the opposite direction of nominal interest rates, has been foreclosed because it leaves one economic policy goal, either economic growth or low inflation, without a dedicated policy instrument. The third part of this chapter tests this hypothesis, finding strong empirical support.

The fourth part then discusses what these results mean for the trade-off between domestic monetary autonomy and exchange rate stability. If a government wishes to achieve exchange rate stability, it must reduce its spending, then permitting lower nominal interest rates in the national economy. Because the world interest rate is low on a nominal basis, lower domestic interest rates produce smaller interest rate differentials (i.e., external monetary policy convergence) and greater external currency stability. But if a government desires to increase its spending, domestic interest rates must correspondingly rise for inflation control. This situation tends to produce larger nominal interest rate differentials (i.e., greater monetary policy autonomy) and increased exchange rate variability.

Understanding this situation helps explain why many OECD governments have asserted domestic monetary autonomy in the form of positive nominal interest rate differentials. They receive many political and economic benefits associated with greater public spending and stand willing to accept the cost in terms of higher national interest rates and reduced exchange rate stability. But governments desiring greater exchange rate stability must also pay certain costs, notably those associated with less government spending. In effect, fiscal policy divergence, defined as the ability of governments to choose their preferred level of public spending, leads to monetary policy divergence—both in terms of domestic interest rates and in terms of exchange rate stability.

I. Policy Goals and Policy Instruments

Models of the domestic political economy often treat governments as if they have only one dominant economic policy goal. Literature on the political business cycle, for example, tends to treat the goal of economic growth and employment as the government's primary policy goal, especially in the run-up to an election. Similarly, the first-wave policy convergence literature focused on low inflation as the government's dominant economic policy goal, downplaying the importance of economic growth.[2] While partisan models of the national political economy often consider both economic growth and low inflation, they tend to assume that leftist (rightist) governments focus on the former (latter) to the exclusion of the latter (former), thus reducing the government's economic policy objectives to a single dominant goal.

The policy mix framework presented in this chapter begins with the idea that all governments must care about both inflation control and economic growth with international capital mobility. Furthermore, the international capital mobility constraint forces them to focus on both economic objectives at the same time. The reason is relatively straightforward. With capital mobility, international investors can move their money in and out of national economies, presumably in search of the highest real returns on investment (see Andrews 1994a; Schulze and Ursprung 1999). Real returns, or real profits, can be roughly defined as nominal returns, or profits, minus inflation losses. Nominal returns tend to increase in a growing economy, which is attractive to international investors. Thus, governments given international capital mobility must be concerned about promoting economic growth. But economic expansion often leads to rising prices. The resulting inflation erodes the real returns on investment, an unattractive result from the perspective of internationally mobile capital.

A couple of examples will illustrate the point that governments must simultaneously promote both economic growth and low inflation. If international investors cared only about economic growth, the flow of money should have been much greater to the global South, where it is not unusual for developing countries to have experienced double-digit rates of growth, often with double-digit rates of inflation.[3] Similarly, if international investors cared only about low inflation, then countries with negative inflation rates (or deflation), such as Japan in the 1990s, should have experienced massive capital inflows. Instead, stagnant growth in Japan led capital to exit that national economy in search of higher returns in Europe and the United States.

The political implications of this economic logic are simple. Governments experiencing the international capital mobility constraint must concurrently pursue two dominant macroeconomic policy goals: economic growth and inflation control. Tending to only one economic policy goal, while ignoring the other (except in the very short term), will induce capital flight, further damag-

2. Emblematic in this regard was the statement of Notermans (1993, 133) that "there is a general consensus amongst policy authorities in the OECD area that macroeconomic policies should have but one goal—the fight against inflation."

3. On the fact that most international capital stays in the global North, see Simmons 1999.

ing the national economy and weakening the government's reelection prospects.

If democratic governments must pursue two domestic macroeconomic objectives, then they will need at least two independent policy instruments to satisfy these goals. Much as a system of equations is "underdetermined" if it contains more variables than equations, economic policy-making usually requires at least as many instruments as goals, according to the famous Tinbergen's Law (see Tinbergen 1966). Mundell (1968, 201) concisely explained: "to achieve a given target [goal] there must be an effective instrument, and to achieve various independent targets there must be at least an equal number of effective instruments. If a program includes more targets than instruments, at least one target cannot be fully attained."

Yet this relationship between the number of policy goals and the number of policy instruments is not true simply by definition. Some policy goals, such as economic growth (the expansion of production) and fuller employment, do tend to be achievable using a single policy instrument, provided that it is properly directed. As national production expands, so do the number of jobs and the employment rate—albeit with some delay. But other policy goals, especially economic growth and low inflation, are much harder to achieve simultaneously using a single policy instrument. This is especially true when economic expansion tends to create rising prices or, at least, the expectation of future inflation.

Policymakers have sometimes expressed economic growth, employment, and inflation as a single-basket policy goal (see Mundell 1968, 204). Implicitly, such an expression makes reference to the Phillips curve, which describes the empirical relationship between employment and inflation in Great Britain from 1861 to 1957 (see Phillips 1958). Phillips's analysis showed that wage inflation increased (or decreased) with the employment (or unemployment) rate. To the extent that the relationship between employment and inflation is one-dimensional (a curve or line has only one dimension), policymakers would, in theory, need only a single policy instrument to achieve their desired combination of growth, employment, and inflation.

The problem for national policymakers is that growth, employment, and inflation outcomes have not fallen along the so-called Phillips curve for most of the post–Bretton Woods era. Stagflation (economic recession with high unemployment and high inflation), experienced by many OECD states in the mid-1970s and then again in the early 1980s, cast considerable empirical doubt on the simple Phillips curve relationship, while the monetarist revolution in economics (see M. Friedman 1968; Phelps 1968) expressed strong theoretical skepticism. If economic growth and inflation outcomes are better understood in two-dimensional space, then policymakers in the post–Bretton Woods era required at least two independent policy instruments to achieve simultaneously the policy goals of economic growth with low inflation. One policy instrument needed to be directed at economic growth, while the other policy instrument was directed at inflation control.

On this point, governments possess two main instruments for economic policy-making: fiscal and monetary policy.[4] Economists define the policy mix as the combination of fiscal and monetary policy choices made by government actors. It is common to treat these two policy instruments as either "tight" or "loose," but I will avoid using these adjectives, because they are too broad for my purposes here and have implications beyond the arguments that I wish to make. For reasons that will become clearer later, I focus on the expenditure side of fiscal policy, not on the revenue side. Thus, my primary fiscal policy measure is government expenditures relative to gross domestic product (GDP). As discussed in chapter 3, my primary monetary policy indicator is short-term policy interest rate in nominal terms.

At this point, it is important to acknowledge that these operational indicators are certainly not the only ways to measure the government's fiscal and monetary policy mix. Political scientists tend to operationalize a government's fiscal policy in terms of its budget deficits, but this has not been the preferred measure for economists when trying to link fiscal policy instruments to particular economic outcomes, as I will be doing here. On this point, Levine and Renelt (1992) reviewed the economics literature on the determinants of long-run economic growth, reporting that government consumption expenditures, total government expenditures, and the budget balance have been the main fiscal policy indicators, in declining order of preference. This preference for spending measures over the budget balance stems from the fact that governments directly control their spending on goods and services through a usually annual appropriation process (see Melitz 2000). But governments have less direct control over the budget balance due to uncertainly regarding tax rev-

---

4. While political leaders theoretically possess other policy instruments, the independence and effectiveness of these instruments is very limited. Take, for example, the so-called instrument of commercial policy, which consists of export subsidies and import restrictions. At some level, export subsidies—government spending targeted on the exporting sector—can be understood as a simple extension of fiscal policy; hence, commercial policy may be nonindependent from fiscal policy. Even if independent, commercial policy may be relatively ineffective, as governments' ability to employ import restrictions has been limited by the World Trade Organization's rules concerning free trade. Similarly, the Mundell-Fleming framework clearly demonstrates how exchange rate policy cannot be separated at all from the monetary policy instrument given international capital mobility; hence, exchange rate policy has been completely nonindependent from monetary policy in the post–Bretton Woods era.

enues and the future state of the national economy. In this sense, budget deficits, much like public debt, are more akin to a policy outcome and less like a policy instrument. I will return to this point later.

On the monetary side, the short-term policy interest rate, not the money supply, serves as the basic instrument of national monetary policy (see Melitz 2000). When monetary authorities want to manipulate the money supply, they tend to use a short-term policy interest rate for this purpose. The money supply thus becomes endogenous to the policy interest rate. Furthermore, as Leertouwer and Maier (2002, 212) wrote, "short-term interest rates could be viewed as capturing the 'net effect' or the sum of all monetary instruments."

2.   The Fiscal and Monetary Policy Mix

Using the relative government spending and nominal interest rate indicators, figure 10 illustrates four possible fiscal and monetary policy mixes. Although illustrated as discrete choices for convenience, it should be obvious that both dimensions (government spending and nominal interest rates) represent a continuum of policy choices. The need to target simultaneously two different and somewhat competing economic policy goals (economic growth and low inflation) given international capital mobility suggests that OECD governments in the post–Bretton Woods era are likely to have gravitated to the policy mixes defined by cells 2 or 3—or, more correctly, into the continuum defined by the off-diagonal—in figure 10.

Each of these two different policy mix choices, or combinations of spending and interest rates, assigns a single policy instrument to a different policy goal— either economic growth or inflation control. If a government increases its spending for economic growth, monetary policy must become its dedicated instrument for inflation control, with higher nominal interest rates to promote domestic price stability and counter inflationary expectations (cell 2). Conversely, if a government chooses to spend less for inflation control,[5] it must lower interest rates to promote economic growth (cell 3).

The fiscal and monetary combinations in cells 1 and 4 may largely be relics of the Bretton Woods system, when capital flows could be restricted. With international capital mobility, using both government spending and interest rates to achieve a single policy goal (either economic growth or low inflation), while neglecting the other, risks capital flight. Except during a deep recession, more government spending with low interest rates (cell 1) will be unattractive

---

5. On how the inflation rate can be potentially manipulated by fiscal policy, see O. Eckstein 1980; Jankowski and Wleizen 1993.

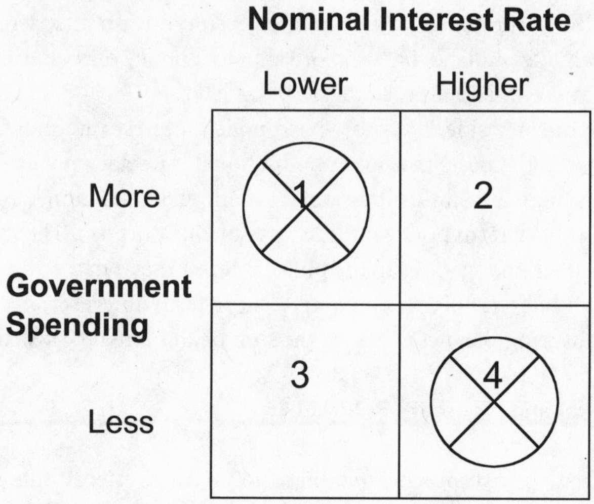

Nominal Interest Rate

Fig. 10.   Different Fiscal and Monetary Policy Mixes

to international capital, as unchecked economic expansion potentially leads to rising prices, with inflation eroding the real returns for capital within the national economy. Similarly, less government spending with high nominal interest rates (cell 4) will be unattractive to international capital except during periods of high inflation, as the policy mix portends a strong economic contraction with expected low returns (both nominal and real) in the national economy.

This policy mix logic can be more formally illustrated as a strategic game between elected governments, who make the annual spending decisions and, thus, control the fiscal policy instrument, and the governments' central bankers, who choose the nominal interest rate and, thus, hold the monetary policy instrument. This game is diagrammed in figure 11. Both players have two strategy options: to expand or to contract their respective policy instrument. With regard to player preferences, I begin with the notion that central banks function as agents of the government. Hence, both players have relatively harmonious preferences for achieving economic growth with low inflation. Thus, the outcome of moderate economic growth with low inflation is preferred to either the outcome of high economic growth with high inflation or the outcome of no economic growth with no inflation.[6]

6. With regard to the choice between high growth with high inflation and no growth with no inflation, governments are likely to prefer the former for electoral reasons, while central banks are likely to prefer the latter, given their mission to guarantee domestic price stability.

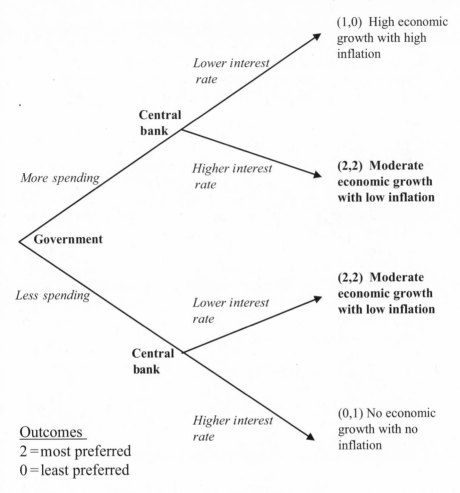

Fig. 11.   The Fiscal and Monetary Strategic Game

At this point, I make no particular distinction between independent and subordinate central banks; nor do I differentiate between the preferences of rightist and leftist governments. These institutional and partisan distinctions will be discussed in chapter 5. In this most basic version of the game, I also make no distinctions about the relative effectiveness of fiscal versus monetary policy for either economic growth or inflation control. Provided that it is properly directed, both instruments are assumed to be equally effective for achieving the policy goal at which they are targeted.

The literature on economic globalization and OECD government spending, as discussed in the previous chapters, clearly demonstrates that the advanced industrial democracies can still make meaningful fiscal policy choices even with international capital mobility (hence, fiscal policy divergence has occurred in the post–Bretton Woods era). If the government chooses to spend more for economic growth, then the central bank can be expected to raise nominal interest rates to restrain inflation. This set of choices results in the policy mix of more government spending and higher nominal interest rates (cell 2 in fig. 10), which is expected to generate moderate economic growth with low inflation. This macroeconomic outcome is preferred by both actors to the alternative of high growth with correspondingly high inflation, produced by more government spending with a lower nominal interest rate.

Alternatively, the government could opt to reduce its spending for inflation control. With less relative spending, the central bank becomes willing to lower nominal interest rates to boost economic growth. This set of choices produces the policy mix of less government spending with a lower nominal interest rate (cell 3 in fig. 10), which is also expected to generate moderate economic growth with low inflation. This macroeconomic outcome is preferred by both actors to the alternative of no economic growth with no inflation, resulting from less government spending with a higher nominal interest rate.

3. Testing the Policy Mix Framework

To be certain, the strategic game described in the preceding section of this chapter represents a very stylized version of national economic policy-making with an international capital mobility constraint. But this stylization has its advantages in presenting a simple and testable hypothesis with regard to the relationship between government spending and nominal interest rates in the OECD economies after 1973. The hypothesis concerns deliberate monetary counterbalancing in response to government spending. If the government spends more, presumably to promote economic growth, then the central bank will raise nominal interest rates for domestic price stability. If the government reduces its spending to minimize inflationary pressures and expectations, then the central bank will lower nominal interest rates, helping to promote economic growth. Although this is an important hypothesis concerning national economic policy-making in the post–Bretton Woods era, it is also an untested one. As Favero (2002, 1) recently noted, while "there is plenty of evidence on the behaviour of monetary policy authorities" and "some evidence on the behaviour of fiscal authorities," "there is very little evidence on the interactions between monetary and fiscal authorities" who control the main two national policy instruments.

To capture as directly as possible the concept of deliberate monetary policy counterbalancing, I will model the policy interest rate for country i in year t (INTRATE), using the same OECD country-year sample that I used in chapter 3.[7] With this goal in mind, the policy interest rate is preferable to any market interest rate, which is determined by the joint activities of mostly private sector actors, not the public sector actors under study here. The base model is laid out in equation (4.1).

$$INTRATE_{it} = \beta_0 + \beta_1{}^*FISCAL_{it} + \alpha_i{}^*COUNTRY_i + \alpha_t{}^*YEAR_t + e_{it} \qquad (4.1)$$

The independent variable FISCAL could be any number of possible fiscal policy measures, including government expenditures, the budget deficit, or even public debt. But as discussed earlier, my policy mix framework focuses on government spending as the preferred measure of a government's fiscal policy intentions. Budget deficits (measured as the difference between government expenditures and tax revenues) are problematic in this regard, as they can vary for reasons unrelated to a government's policy intentions.[8] Stone and Sawhill (1984, 44) wrote, "It is now widely recognized that changes in the actual budget deficit are a poor measure of changes in the thrust of fiscal policy, because the budget is sensitive to the level of economic activity as well as to policy changes." A public debt measure for the current national fiscal policy orientation is even more problematic, as it reflects choices made by numerous past governments, rather than the present one.

In choosing a spending measure to capture most directly the deliberate fiscal policy choice made by current governments, not all spending measures will be equally valid. Total government spending can be roughly broken down

7. The policy interest rate data was also described in chapter 3.

8. For certain governments, they may be a completely misleading indicator of their fiscal policy intentions. For example, Reagan administration officials viewed their tax cuts, which led to massive budget deficits, as a strategy for long-term fiscal policy contraction. This political perspective, not unique to the Reagan administration, reverses the traditional economic logic about tax cuts as a tool for fiscal expansion. Weatherford and McDonnell (1990, 145) concluded, "for most of his administration, Reagan viewed deficit reduction as a lever he could use to further his goal of decreasing domestic expenditures." Johnson (1998, 185) reported, "Stockman [Reagan's director of the Office of Management and Budget] believed that he could browbeat the cabinet into major program rollbacks by holding out tax cuts—and Volcker's reductions in interest rates—as a reward for pruning spending." Stockman (1986, 68) himself wrote: "the prospect of needing well over $100 billion in domestic spending cuts to keep the Republican budget in equilibrium appeared more as an opportunity than as a roadblock. Once . . . Reagan got an electoral mandate for Kemp-Roth and 10–5–3 [two major tax cut plans], then we would have the Second Republic's craven politicians [Congress controlled by Democratic interest groups] pinned to the wall. They would have to dismantle its bloated, wasteful, and unjust spending enterprises—or risk national ruin."

into three component categories: government consumption, social transfers, and interest payments. The latter two categories are essentially obligatory in nature; that is, governments cannot easily change their spending habits with regard to either transfers or interest payments, especially in the short term as hypothesized here. Furthermore, the level of spending in these obligatory categories largely reflects spending decisions made by past governments and then imposed on the one currently in power. To the extent that it is possible to capture current discretionary spending, government consumption relative to GDP is arguably the most valid spending measure. This category includes current spending on such goods and services as public administration, public order, national defense, health, and education. Thus, FISCAL indicates government consumption expenditures, in constant terms, as a percent of country i's GDP in year t.[9] Higher (or lower) values generally suggest a more expansionary (or contractionary) fiscal policy orientation in constant terms.

My counterbalancing hypothesis predicts that the FISCAL coefficient will be positively signed and statistically significant. When OECD governments have chosen to spend more to promote economic growth, national monetary authorities have raised interest rates for inflation control. To the extent that OECD governments have simply focused on a single domestic policy goal— either economic growth or low inflation—and have used both monetary and fiscal policies at the same time toward this goal, the FISCAL coefficient will be negatively signed and statistically significant. Finally, if OECD governments have made no efforts at all to coordinate their fiscal and monetary policies in any consistent fashion, then the FISCAL coefficient will simply be statistically insignificant.

Just as in the set of time-series cross-sectional models presented in the previous chapter, I here use panel-corrected standard errors to deal with panel heteroskedasticity and contemporaneous autocorrelation. To correct for serial autocorrelation in each country time series, I also estimate and adjust for first-order autocorrelation as was done in the previous chapter. Several sets of results, including those with some additional control variables, are shown in table 3.

The estimates for the base model in equation (4.1) are reported in the first column of table 3. Consistent with my counterbalancing hypothesis, the FISCAL coefficient is positively signed and statistically significant. A 1 percent increase in government consumption spending relative to GDP is associated with an increase in the policy interest rate of forty-two basis points. This

9. The data are provided by the OECD in *Annual National Accounts* (1973–97).

finding is consistent with those reported by Melitz (1997, 2000), who found that OECD monetary and fiscal policies move in opposite directions (one contracts while the other expands), with interest rates and government spending acting as "strategic substitutes" (Buti, Roeger, and In't Veld 2001, 3).

I also obtained positive fiscal coefficients when I measured a government's fiscal policy using its relative budget deficit and public debt. But it is not clear that these results shed much light on my research question concerning the deliberate coordination of monetary and fiscal policy instruments. It is already well established that larger deficits and greater debt contribute to higher interest rates in the domestic economy. But this is largely a story of how deficits and debt crowd out private investment, which ultimately tells us little about how the government actors actually holding the monetary and fiscal policy instruments might coordinate them to achieve economic growth with low inflation.

In the second column of table 3, I reestimated the model, adding some

TABLE 3.   Estimates of Government Spending on the Policy Interest Rate

	1	2	3
Constant	−1.75	0.71	2.13
	(2.51)	(3.38)	(3.41)
FISCAL	0.42***	0.33***	0.27**
	(0.13)	(0.12)	(0.12)
GDPGROWTH		0.05	0.04
		(0.11)	(0.10)
INFLATION		0.27***	0.27***
		(0.09)	(0.09)
GDPPC		−0.00052***	−0.00055***
		(0.00014)	(0.00015)
KOPEN		0.54***	0.53***
		(0.20)	(0.20)
EMS			−0.91*
			(0.55)
SNAKE			−0.95
			(0.74)
UNIPEG			0.12
			(0.55)
N	575	575	575
R^2	0.53	0.73	0.72

Note: Estimates are Prais-Winsten coefficients, including an AR1 correction, with panel-corrected standard errors in parentheses. Individual country and year dummies are not reported.

Two-tailed statistical significance is indicated as follows: ***$p < .01$, **$p < .05$, *$p < .10$.

important control variables. To estimate more precisely how much national monetary authorities have increased short-term interest rates with more government spending, it is useful to hold economic growth and inflation rates constant. Thus, I included the variables GDPGROWTH and INFLATION. At the end of chapter 3, I discussed how the level of economic development may affect national interest rates. Thus, I also included the country's GDP per capita (GDPPC) in each year.[10] Finally, I added the control variable for international capital mobility (KOPEN), described in chapter 3. With the addition of these control variables, the FISCAL coefficient is slightly attenuated, but it remains positively signed and statistically significant.

I argued earlier that fixed exchange rate commitments in the post–Bretton Woods era have been only weakly associated with external monetary convergence—due in large part to the flexible operation of such regimes as the European Snake and the EMS and to the inherent flexibility associated with unilateral decisions to peg national currencies. It is valuable to bring some additional evidence to bear on the subject. Thus, in the third column of table 3, I added to the model the EMS, SNAKE, and UNIPEG dummy variables, all of which are described in chapter 3.

Chapter 3 also showed how most advanced industrial democracies needed to be able to reduce national interest rates—moving them toward the low world interest rate—in order to achieve external monetary convergence after 1973 (see fig. 8 in chap. 3). Thus, if these various multilateral and unilateral commitments had any strong effects in promoting external monetary policy convergence, the coefficient for each (or some) of these variables should be negative and statistically significant. While EMS and SNAKE have the expected negative sign in table 3, only the EMS coefficient is statistically different from zero, and it is so only at the .10 level.[11] These results are consistent with those in chapter 3, demonstrating how different OECD monetary regimes (both multilateral and unilateral) have had only weak effects in explaining national monetary policy after 1973. Clearly, if we want to understand national monetary policy choices in the post–Bretton Woods era, we get much more explanatory power by looking first at government spending decisions; hence, the policy mix framework is potentially useful.

10. The data for all these control variables come from the World Bank's *World Development Indicators* (1973–97).

11. Weak EMS effects with regard to national interest rates and interest rate differentials have been reported by other scholars. For example, Marston (1995, 136) concluded: "uncovered interest [rate] differentials persist among the major European countries. In fact, departures from uncovered interest parity within the EMS are as large on average as those between EMS and non-EMS currencies."

Finally, the statistically significant negative coefficient on the GDPPC term in table 3 demonstrates another important fact: monetary convergence vis-à-vis the most developed capitalist economies will almost always require a lower nominal interest rate, since more developed OECD states naturally have lower rates. Shambaugh's recent results in the economics literature (2004, 320–21) paint a very similar picture: national interest rate differentials have been quite positive in the post–Bretton Woods era relative to the so-called base countries ($i > i^*$), even for the advanced industrial democracies. External monetary convergence thus necessitated a lower national interest rate.

4. The Policy Mix and Exchange Rate Stability

To summarize briefly before incorporating the issue of exchange rate stability into the policy mix framework, the preceding analysis has demonstrated how OECD governments have gravitated toward a particular policy mix continuum in the post–Bretton Woods era. When fiscal policy became more expansive (as measured by more government spending relative to GDP), nominal interest rates also rose, leading to a policy mix of more government spending with a higher nominal interest rate. When government spending became more contractionary, the nominal interest rate fell, resulting in a policy mix of less government spending with a lower nominal interest rate.

The theoretical foundations for this fiscal and monetary relationship concern the government's need to use public spending and interest rates to satisfy simultaneously two different—and often difficult to reconcile—internal economic policy goals: economic growth and low inflation. In the policy mix framework just presented, the external policy goal of exchange rate stability does not have its own independent policy instrument. But I submit that this is not a problem with the theoretical framework. Indeed, it reflects an important macroeconomic policy reality: national policymakers lack a separate and independent policy instrument for the purpose of exchange rate stabilization in the post–Bretton Woods era of international capital mobility (see Moses 1994, 133).

But this fact does not mean that this external policy goal will be impossible to achieve with global financial integration. Governments seeking relative exchange rate stability vis-à-vis the most developed capital-producing states in the international system (i.e., those who effectively set the world interest rate) can choose the policy mix of less government spending and a lower nominal interest rate (see fig. 12). Less government spending permits the nominal interest rate to fall, bringing the domestic interest rate toward the low prevailing

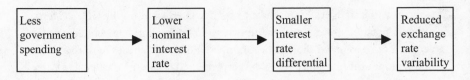

Fig. 12.   Internal Policy Choices Leading to External Policy Convergence

world rate. Such external monetary policy convergence, or a smaller interest rate differential, helps reduce exchange rate variability, as was demonstrated empirically in table 2 in chapter 3. To the extent that neoliberal policy ideas prescribe reduced government intervention in the national economy and more stable exchange rates,[12] the combination of less government spending and a lower nominal interest rate might be described as the neoliberal policy mix.

This understanding accords with the expectations for external policy convergence in Western Europe in the 1990s. The 1992 Maastricht Agreement, often described as neoliberal in its policy orientation, specified five convergence criteria, which might be described simply as (1) lower inflation, (2) lower budget deficits, (3) reduced public debt, (4) lower national interest rates, and (5) exchange rate stability within the exchange rate mechanism of the EMS (see Watson 1997). For lower national inflation rates, EU governments were expected to curtail their spending in order to reduce budget deficits and public debt. Such fiscal contraction was, in turn, expected to facilitate a reduction in national interest rates, so that they would converge on those of the low-inflation economies (especially Germany) in the European Union. This combination of fiscal contraction and lower nominal interest rates was then expected to help stabilize national currency values within the EMS before the shift to a common European currency in 1999.

While it brings greater exchange rate stability, this neoliberal policy mix also entails important costs, especially those related to fiscal policy contraction. One significant drawback with reduced government spending is that public goods in the national economy may become undersupplied. Fiscal contraction also reduces the government's opportunities for redistribution designed to reduce income inequalities. But if the government increases its spending for these purposes, the nominal interest rate and the interest rate differential can be expected to rise correspondingly (see fig. 13). These results are quite consis-

12. On the connection between neoliberal policy ideas and exchange rate stability, see McNamara 1998.

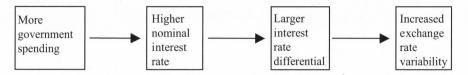

Fig. 13.   Internal Policy Choices Leading to Domestic Policy Autonomy

tent with those reported by Mosley (2000, 762), who showed that OECD governments have paid an interest rate premium for engaging in more spending across a variety of spending categories, including government consumption, the primary fiscal policy measure used in this study.

It has not been previously recognized, however, that paying these interest rate premiums effectively represents a choice for domestic monetary autonomy, given financial integration among the OECD states in the post–Bretton Woods era. In other words, these interest rate premiums demonstrate the price that many governments have been willing to pay in an effort to achieve particular domestic economic objectives through fiscal policy expansion. This price also comes in the form of increased exchange rate variability: the results in chapter 3 show how greater monetary policy independence in the form of a larger interest rate differential has produced more external currency instability after 1973. Thus, of the two fiscal and monetary policy mixes available to OECD governments in the post–Bretton Woods era, the combination of less government spending with a lower nominal interest rate represents a choice for external policy convergence and exchange rate stability, as illustrated in figure 14. Conversely, the policy mix of more government spending with a higher nominal interest rate effectively signals a choice for domestic policy autonomy with correspondingly more exchange rate variability.

At this point, the reader should note that I have deliberately shifted away from the term *domestic monetary policy autonomy* to the term *domestic policy autonomy*. Similarly, I will shift from the term *external monetary policy convergence* to the term *external policy convergence*. This change is not accidental: the policy mix framework shows how the choice for exchange rate stability with international capital mobility implicates not only domestic monetary policy but fiscal policy as well. This possibility has been suggested by other scholars (see, e.g., Simmons 1999, 36; Garrett 2000, 166), but without an explicit model to explain the linkage from fiscal policy through monetary policy to exchange rate stability. The policy mix framework fills this important theoretical gap. In doing so, it provides a relatively simple and tractable model of national eco-

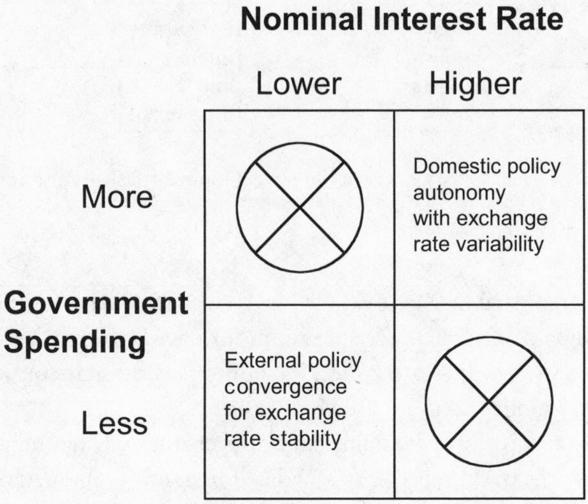

Nominal Interest Rate

Lower   Higher

More

Domestic policy
autonomy
with exchange
rate variability

**Government
Spending**

Less

External policy
convergence
for exchange
rate stability

Fig. 14.   Exchange Rate Stability and the Policy Mix

nomic policy-making that integrates government spending, national interest rates, and exchange rate stability into a common theoretical framework.

The policy mix framework also forces us to think more carefully about the relationship between fiscal policy and exchange rate stability. The traditional logic, borrowed from the Mundell-Fleming model and recently applied to the political business cycle literature (see Clark and Hallerberg 2000; Clark 2002, 2003), begins with fixed exchange rates and concludes with a more effective national fiscal policy. The standard Mundell-Fleming logic is that since fiscal policy expansion raises domestic interest rates, national monetary authorities must accommodate increased government spending with lower interest rates in order to restore the interest parity condition and maintain fixed exchange rates. If fixed exchange rates are thus maintained, then fiscal expansion becomes a highly effective policy instrument for stimulating the national economy, because it produces an accompanying monetary expansion.

In the basic Mundell-Fleming model, this monetary accommodation is unproblematic, since prices are assumed to be fixed and since fiscal expansion produces no inflationary effects. But in the real world, such monetary accommodation is problematic, since prices are not fixed and since fiscal expansion can have significant inflationary implications. The logic that allows researchers to reason that fixed exchange rates lead to fiscal policy expansion is also problematic in taking exchange rate stability as a given, exogenous to domestic monetary and fiscal policy decisions. Furthermore, political science applications take it as a given based on a government's stated commitment to fix its exchange rate (i.e., its de jure exchange rate regime). The analysis presented here shows how such stated commitments are only weakly associated with reduced currency variability and external monetary policy convergence.

We cannot treat a national exchange rate as fixed simply because the government declares it to be so. The policy mix framework demonstrates how a government must make internal policy decisions that are consistent with external currency stability in order to achieve fixed or more stable exchange rates. Given the fiscal and monetary counterbalancing conducted by OECD governments in the post–Bretton Woods era, more government spending may be largely inconsistent with de facto fixed exchange rates.[13] Instead of lowering interest rates after fiscal expansion to achieve smaller interest rate differentials (i.e., monetary accommodation), OECD monetary authorities have tended to raise them for domestic inflation control, leading to larger interest rate differentials and destabilizing capital flows.

This understanding nicely explains why European exchange rate regimes began to operate as fiscal policy constraints after 1992. As mentioned earlier, EU governments adopted the Maastricht convergence criteria in 1992, which—among other things—required prospective EMU member states to reduce budget deficits to no more than 3 percent of GDP and public debt to no more than 60 percent of GDP, potentially constraining their spending options. In 1997, the prospective EMU member states further concluded the Stability and Growth Pact, which made governments running budget deficits in excess of 3 percent of GDP potentially subject to huge fines (up to 0.5 percent of GDP).

Researchers using the traditional logic that equates exchange rate stability with opportunities for fiscal policy expansion have trouble explaining these facts. After all, why should governments agree to constrain their national fiscal policy if the whole point of the fixed exchange rate regime was to make their fiscal policy instrument more effective? The policy mix framework, which begins with the internal fiscal and monetary policy decisions made by national governments in order to explain their external currency (in)stability, can explain these facts. Governments achieve greater exchange rate stability, or de facto fixity, when they reduce their spending, allowing nominal interest rates to fall and minimizing the national interest rate differential vis-à-vis the low world interest rate. Consequently, when governments join fixed exchange rate

13. For additional evidence on this point, see Froot and Rogoff 1991; Healy 2004; Bearce 2005.

regimes to enable their fiscal policy instrument and engage in more spending, they are likely to find that exchange rate stability will be very hard, if not impossible, to achieve. But if a major reason for these monetary regimes (if not the primary one) was to increase regional exchange rate stability (Frieden 2002), the participating governments had to acknowledge that fiscal expansion was ultimately counterproductive to this end. Hence, they agreed to fiscal policy constraints in an effort to achieve more fixed exchange rates.

This policy mix logic can also help explain the historical disconnect between many governments' stated currency commitments, or their de jure exchange rate regimes, and the actual stability of their national currency, or their de facto exchange rate regimes (Reinhart and Rogoff 2004). If a government makes an external commitment to fix its currency's value but follows a domestic fiscal and monetary policy mix expected to increase the interest rate differential and exacerbate external currency variability, then it is not hard to understand why there would be a large discrepancy between exchange rate "words and deeds" (Levy-Yeyati and Sturzenegger 2005). Likewise, we can better understand why certain governments without any formal commitments to fix the value of their national currencies nonetheless achieved relative external currency stability (Calvo and Reinhart 2002): they followed an internal policy mix that reduced national interest rate differentials and facilitated a more fixed exchange rate.

CHAPTER 5

Explaining Divergence
in the Policy Mix

In the preceding chapters, I have shown that monetary policy divergence, linked to the phenomenon of fiscal policy divergence, best describes the post–Bretton Woods era. A second research question must now be addressed. How can we explain these related patterns of policy divergence among the OECD countries after 1973? Restated, using the language of the Mundell-Fleming framework, what factors led many national governments to choose domestic policy autonomy, accepting the loss of exchange rate stability? Similarly, what factors led other governments to choose exchange rate stability, sacrificing the benefits of domestic policy autonomy?

These questions are important and have not been satisfactorily answered. Pauly (1995, 386) once wrote: "under what conditions do powerful and potentially dominant states voluntarily relinquish policy autonomy? This remains a key question for future research in this area." Cohen (1996, 283–84) similarly stated: "The interesting question . . . is not whether financial globalization imposes a constraint on sovereign states; it most clearly does. Rather, we should now be asking how the discipline works and under what conditions." He continued: "The number of conditions that might influence the preferred trade-off between policy autonomy and exchange rate stability is quite large. What is needed is more careful and applied investigation of how each works in today's financially integrated world" (285).

To begin this investigation, it is useful to take one step back and briefly review. Chapter 4 demonstrated how OECD governments have moved their fiscal and monetary policy instruments in opposite directions in the post–Bretton Woods era. Consequently, these governments have moved onto the policy mix continuum defined by more government spending with a higher interest rate at one end and less government spending with a lower interest rate at the other end. Chapter 4 also showed how domestic policy autonomy in the post–Bretton Woods era has been defined by movement toward the first end: more government spending led to higher national interest rates and larger interest rate differentials, resulting in greater exchange rate variability (see fig. 15). Conversely, governments who desired external policy convergence for exchange rate stability moved toward the other end: less government spending permitted a lower national interest rate, which, in turn, facilitated a smaller interest rate differential and reduced external currency variability.

Understanding a government's preferred trade-off between domestic policy autonomy and exchange rate stability thus requires an explanation of its policy mix choice. This chapter will proceed on that basis. Although the number of conditions that might influence the policy mix choice and, therefore, the trade-off between domestic policy autonomy and external currency stability is certainly large, the analysis here will focus primarily on the role of government partisanship.

I focus on government partisanship because it is a factor posited as relatively unimportant by different convergence theories. As discussed in chapter 2, the first wave of macroeconomic policy convergence theory argued that international capital mobility and, more broadly, economic globalization constrained partisan economic policy differences in the post–Bretton Woods era (see, e.g., Garrett and Lange 1991; Kurzer 1993). While Garrett (1995, 1998b) and other scholars later demonstrated growing fiscal policy divergence with greater capital and trade openness, their results have recently been challenged by a new partisan convergence thesis offered by Clark (2003). According to Clark's argument, it is not economic globalization that constrains partisan policy differences; instead, partisan economic policy convergence simply emerges from democratic capitalism (hence, Clark titled his 2003 book *Capitalism, Not Globalism*).

Thus, the ball has been solidly hit back to the partisan divergence side of the court. For scholars still positing partisan economic policy differences in the post–Bretton Woods era, it has now become especially important to establish more precisely why and where one should expect to see them. It is also important to establish where partisan policy divergence would not be expected to occur in the post–Bretton Woods era. Partisan differences in terms of main economic policy instruments do not necessarily imply partisan divergence in terms of dominant economic policy goals, just as partisan convergence in terms of policy goals does not force partisan convergence with regard to policy instruments.

While I focus on the role of government partisanship in explaining economic policy divergence, I also consider the role of two other factors: political

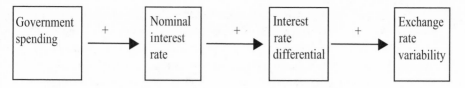

Fig. 15.   Linking Fiscal Policy, Monetary Policy, and Exchange Rate Stability

power-sharing and central bank independence. This chapter thus proceeds in five sections. The first three sections examine the domestic political factors (government partisanship, political power-sharing, and central bank independence) in order, making a series of hypotheses. The fourth section tests the hypotheses about how these factors influence government spending, national interest rates, the extent of domestic monetary autonomy, and the stability of the national currency's value. The strongest statistical results emerge for government partisanship. Thus, the fifth section discusses how these results lead us toward a new and more nuanced theory of partisan economic policy-making in the post–Bretton Woods era.

1. Government Partisanship

As presented in chapter 4, the policy mix choice was motivated solely by the need to satisfy simultaneously the two domestic macroeconomic goals of economic growth and low inflation. But partisan governments have other economic policy objectives to varying degrees, including the provision of public goods, income redistribution, and exchange rate stability. The strategic game modeled in figure 11 in chapter 4 suggested that governments would be largely indifferent—at least in terms of economic growth and low inflation policy outcomes—in choosing between the policy mix of more government spending with a higher nominal interest rate, on the one hand, and the alternative mix of less government spending with a lower nominal interest rate. However, partisan governments are likely not so indifferent in actual practice, because they must try to meet other economic priorities using one of these two fiscal and monetary combinations. In general, I expect that leftist governments have been more likely to choose the policy mix associated with domestic policy autonomy, while rightist governments have moved toward the alternative for external policy convergence with exchange rate stability.

This hypothesis begins with the understanding that monetary and fiscal expansion do not serve as perfect substitutes. While both may promote aggregate economic growth, fiscal expansion is better suited than monetary expansion for income redistribution and public goods provision. With regard to income redistribution, this is true because monetary adjustments tend to affect the economy as a whole (see Gowa 1988); thus, targeting particular societal groups may be difficult to achieve with a cut in interest rates. While cheaper money may eventually produce more jobs for and raise the wages of lower-income groups, the initial impact of a monetary expansion is likely to benefit higher-income groups, those qualifying most easily to borrow money for their business ventures. Indeed, monetary expansion may even increase income inequality in the short run, before its benefits trickle down to lower-income groups.

However, fiscal expansion is well suited for income redistribution, as it can be targeted to benefit lower-income societal groups (see Hallerberg 2002, 782). Fiscal expansion may also be necessary for increasing public goods. Additional government spending can fund better public schools, improvements in the national infrastructure, and greater research and development for public purposes. Conversely, while monetary expansion facilitates private investment, most of the goods created through private investment are unlikely ever to become available on a purely public basis. With this understanding in mind, we can now consider the fiscal and monetary policy pressures that various societal interest groups apply on different political parties.

Interest Group Pressures on Political Parties

Scholars studying partisan politics in the advanced industrial economies have long been comfortable in identifying leftist parties as agents for labor interests in society (see, e.g., Garrett 1995) and identifying rightist parties as agents for capital interests, following cleavages along factors of production (or classes). While some scholars have suggested a decline in class-based partisan politics, various studies presented by Evans (1999) demonstrate how socioeconomic position remains a significant predictor of party support in the advanced industrial democracies. With this understanding, what might be labor's interest with regard to the policy mix?

As it is more fixed in the domestic economy than is mobile capital,[1] relatively immobile labor can be expected to have stronger preferences for the local

---

1. On this point, see Schulze and Ursprung 1999, 298. Even in the European Union, where the movement of labor across national borders is permitted, labor mobility tends to be quite low, due especially to European cultural and linguistic differences. Most non-European states maintain controls on labor mobility, as do EU states with regard to non-EU labor.

public goods provided through greater government spending. As labor also stands to benefit from income redistribution, it can be expected to favor fiscal, over monetary, expansion. If more government spending becomes the dedicated instrument for economic growth to achieve greater public goods and income redistribution, monetary policy must be used for inflation control, resulting in higher nominal interest rates. Interestingly, high interest rates may benefit labor beyond simple domestic price stability. When interest rates are high, acquiring capital becomes more costly, and costly capital may lead certain businesses to substitute cheaper labor for the capital inputs to their production, thus creating jobs in the local economy.[2]

As discussed in chapter 4, the obvious cost of this policy mix is exchange rate instability, as national interest rates move farther away from the low world interest rate (i.e., domestic monetary autonomy as defined by a larger interest rate differential). On this point, however, it is interesting to note that currency variability may provide some unexpected benefits to labor. If exchange rate instability raises the cost of moving capital out of the domestic economy due to increased external investment risk and the expense of purchasing forward-exchange contracts to hedge against this risk, capital may be more likely to remain in the local economy, helping to provide jobs and income for labor.[3]

Perhaps not surprisingly, capital interests allied with the political right can be expected to favor the alternative policy mix of less government spending with a lower nominal interest rate for greater exchange rate stability. Since it is less tied to the domestic economy than immobile labor, mobile capital should be correspondingly less interested in local public goods, especially if taxes must be raised to pay for these public goods. Similarly, many capital holders can be expected to oppose increased government spending for the purposes of income redistribution toward labor. Thus, it is not hard to see how decreased government spending may be capital's preferred means of maintaining low inflation. Of course, capital is also interested in economic growth, but monetary expansion is likely to be its preferred policy instrument, especially as lower interest rates facilitate private investment opportunities. As the national interest rate falls, moving closer to the low world interest rate (i.e., external monetary convergence), capital will be further advantaged by reduced external currency vari-

2. On this point, see *Economist* 2004c.

3. This logic suggests how currency volatility may function as a de facto capital control, discouraging financial capital from exiting the domestic economy in search of potentially higher external returns, which might exist absent such costly currency volatility. Scholars have already demonstrated that leftist parties embraced de jure capital controls more willingly than did rightist parties (see Grilli and Milesi-Ferretti 1995; Quinn and Inclan 1997).

ability. As mentioned earlier, exchange rate instability potentially adds risk to making external investments. Of course, capital holders might purchase forward-exchange contracts to hedge against such currency risk, but these contracts are costly and erode capital's returns on its external investments.

Having just argued for partisan fiscal and monetary policy differences using a factor- and class-based Heckscher-Ohlin model, I can also make a similar hypothesis about partisan divergence using the Ricardo-Viner model, which presents a sectoral framework. There has been a tendency in the political economy literature to treat the Heckscher-Ohlin and the Ricardo-Viner models as substitutes (see, e.g., Alt et al. 1996). But as Fordham and McKeown (2003, 522) persuasively argued, these two models may be quite complementary: "The presence of sectoral effects is not inconsistent with the presence of factoral effects. The standard neoclassical theory holds that countries export goods that intensively employ their abundant factors. If so, in the United States [for example] the geographic distribution of skilled (unskilled) labor would be correlated with that of exporting (import-competing) sectors. If exporters employed no unskilled labor, and import-competing firms employed no skilled labor, the correlation would be perfect."[4]

On this basis, it is not at all surprising to observe sectoral-partisan affiliations. As Esping-Andersen (1999, 311) recently noted, traditional class-political cleavages "are being overlaid by new kinds of 'class' politics," with leftist parties drawing their support from the sheltered public sector and the middle-class white-collar service sector. Similarly, rightist parties in the advanced industrial democracies have relatively tight political links to banks and financial service firms, as well as to the large multinational corporations who conduct the bulk of international trade and foreign direct investment (see Silk and Vogel 1977; Jacobs 1999).

These sectoral-partisan affiliations have been particularly pronounced in the United States since the late 1970s, although they are certainly not limited to this political economy, as the case studies in chapter 6 will demonstrate. Dissatisfied with the Carter administration's autonomous policy stance, American banking and multinational firms withdrew what little support they had provided to the Democrats, helping the Republicans to regain the presidency in 1980 (see Ferguson and Rogers 1986, 113). Indeed, U.S. big business contributed significantly more to Republicans than to Democrats during the

4. On this point, one identifies such industries as steel and textiles in the developed world as part of the import-competing sector, rather than as part of the international exporting sector, because their heavy manual labor inputs render them almost noncompetitive in international markets dominated by lower-cost producers from the developing world.

1979–80 election cycle (Ryan, Swanson, and Buchholz 1987, 132). On this point, Himmelstein (1990, 129) wrote how American big business "moved to the right in the 1970s, emphasizing the pivotal role of 'capital-intensive industries [exporters], investment banks, and internationally oriented commercial banks' in shaping American politics." Providing quantitative data to support the electoral connection between the Republican Party and internationally oriented voters, as well as that between the Democratic Party and domestically oriented voters, Hout, Manza, and Brooks (1999) showed that skilled manual workers (likely to be found in export-oriented industries, as U.S. companies export from a comparative advantage in skilled labor) have shifted their support toward the Republicans. Furthermore, they documented how professional and routine white-collar workers in the largely nontradable service sector increasingly support the Democrats, as do less-skilled manual workers (likely trapped in the import-competing manufacturing sector).

As Frieden (1991, 445) described, domestically oriented sectors of the national economy hold stronger preferences for domestic policy autonomy than for exchange rate stability. This is true because producers of import-competing goods and nontradable services conduct relatively little international business; thus, they receive few immediate benefits from currency stability. Inasmuch as domestic policy autonomy includes greater government spending (as discussed in chapter 4), these domestically oriented sectors stand to benefit from the local public goods provided through such fiscal policy expansion. Monetary expansion, as the alternative growth strategy, leaves such public goods either undersupplied or supplied in a private form inaccessible to many firms confined to the domestic economy.

Since inflation hurts almost all business activity, even import-competing manufacturing and those in the service sector have an interest in domestic price stability. But benefiting as they do from fiscal expansion, these domestically oriented sectors likely prefer inflation control through monetary, rather than fiscal, contraction. As Garrett and Lange (1995, 648) noted, the "combination of loose fiscal policies and tight monetary policies would greatly benefit the nontradables sector." Furthermore, the exchange rate instability associated with this autonomous policy mix also benefits import-competing producers, as currency variability tends to increase the transaction costs of their import competition, thus raising the price of imported goods and making domestically produced goods appear less expensive in the home market.

Inasmuch as leftist parties may be pressured toward domestic policy autonomy through their representation of labor-intensive domestically oriented business sectors, rightist parties should be pushed toward external policy convergence and exchange rate stability by capital-intensive internationally oriented sectors. As Frieden (1991, 445) described, exporters and international investors can be expected to favor exchange rate stability over domestic policy autonomy, since the currency risk associated with moving goods and money across international borders can be eliminated if exchange rates remain fixed over time.

The policy mix of less government spending with a lower nominal interest rate that is associated with greater exchange rate stability is also attractive for capital-intensive international businesses, as they have little interest in an economic growth strategy through fiscal expansion designed to reduce wealth inequalities and redistribute income. To the extent that international big business desires to get government out of the national economies, reduced public spending becomes a preferred policy instrument for inflation control. With regard to economic growth, internationally oriented sectors of the economy are likely to favor monetary expansion, since lower interest rates tend to increase their investment opportunities by reducing the costs of acquiring additional capital.

In short, whether one prefers to look at interest group preferences divided along either factoral or sectoral lines (or to look at preferences along both lines), leftist parties likely face greater interest group pressure for domestic policy autonomy, while rightist parties are pushed toward external policy convergence for exchange rate stability.[5] However, we should not only expect to see certain partisan economic policy differences on the basis of interest group pressures. We should also expect to observe partisan divergence from differing policy ideas.

Policy Ideas and Political Parties

Few would dispute that leftist political parties began the post–Bretton Woods era as adherents of Keynesian economic ideas. Simply stated, Keynesian policy ideas advised governments to manage the demand side of their national economies, stimulating aggregate demand when economic growth began to stagnate (i.e., they were to use countercyclical demand management). In theory, demand stimulation could come from either fiscal or monetary policy expansion, but Keynesian practice during the Bretton Woods regime demon-

5. For more on how leftist parties act as the partisan agents for domestically oriented producer groups and how rightist parties act as the partisan agents for internationally oriented producer groups, see Bearce 2003.

strated the "asymmetry of monetary policy": "it seemed far easier to restrain than to encourage demand" using interest rates and money supply (Thygesen 1982, 349). Consequently, fiscal, rather than monetary, expansion became the Left's favored policy instrument for stimulating aggregate demand.

The stagflation experience beginning in the early 1970s meant that leftist governments needed a dedicated instrument for inflation control as the post–Bretton Woods era began. With increased government spending directed toward economic expansion, leftist governments predictably used monetary contraction to stabilize domestic prices.[6] Indeed, it was not simply the case that leftist governments passively accepted higher interest rates to fight inflation, one can also find examples of Keynesian-oriented leftist governments actively pushing their central bank for monetary contraction.[7] Kettl (1986, 170) wrote: "[Carter] administration officials had become convinced that OPEC oil price increases made tighter money necessary. They believed [Federal Reserve Board chairman] Miller erred by keeping monetary policy too loose. CEA Chairman Charles Schultze and Treasury Secretary W. Michael Blumenthal . . . began a calculated series of leaks and interviews to pressure the Fed to tighten."[8]

Although Keynesian ideas may have influenced leftist political parties at the beginning of the post–Bretton Woods era, McNamara (1998) argued that the political left accepted a new conservative economic orthodoxy after their poor experience in combating stagflation in the 1970s. In the 1980s, "socialists and conservatives alike," contended McNamara (1998, 10), adopted competitive neoliberal policy ideas, borrowing from monetarist economic theory. These ideas encouraged fiscal discipline, stable growth in the money supply, and even exchange rate stability.[9] Indeed, as discussed in chapter 2, McNamara's argument has become one of the leading explanations for the monetary policy con-

6. This use of monetary policy for inflation control might be termed "pragmatic Keynesianism," consistent with McNamara's distinction (1998, 67–69) between academic monetarism and pragmatic monetarism.

7. A similar example was provided by the Italian Communists' endorsement of higher interest rates in Italy, provided that fiscal policy remained relatively expansionary. Goodman (1992, 159) wrote: "in September 1976, the Communists wholeheartedly endorsed the government's decision to impose a series of restrictive monetary measures. Even more important, the Communists proved willing to accept and sell the new IMF program to the unions."

8. Carter's decision to replace Miller with Paul Volcker accords with this evidence. Karier (1997, 40) wrote on this subject: "the Carter administration well understood the risks posed by Volcker's appointment. The commitment to Paul Volcker was a commitment to tight money."

9. This last point is not obvious, since such monetarists as Milton Friedman were advocates of floating exchange rates (M. Friedman 1953). But McNamara (1998, 67–69) was careful to distinguish between monetarist academic theory, which prescribed floating rates, and pragmatic monetarist ideas, which viewed exchange rate stability as paramount.

vergence that supposedly occurred in Western Europe since the late 1970s: according to this argument, the political left adopted the economic policy ideas espoused by the political right, and this is why European governments of all party types now run very similar economic policy programs.

The problem with this argument is not that OECD governments failed to follow such neoliberal policy ideas in the 1980s. Clearly, many governments did—including the Christian Democrats in West Germany, the Conservatives in Britain, the U.S. Republicans, and the Japanese Liberal Democratic Party (LDP).[10] The problem is that there were relatively few left-wing governments in power during the 1980s, and it is not particularly surprising that the right-wing governments already mentioned would follow such a conservative economic orthodoxy. Indeed, among the economies of the G-7 (the Group of Seven included France, West Germany, Italy, Japan, the United Kingdom, the United States, and Canada), only France was governed by a leftist party for a substantial portion of the 1980s. This fact helps to explain why certain convergence theorists invested so much effort in describing Mitterrand's economic policy as neoliberal in character, especially after the so-called U-turn of 1983.

But as I will demonstrate in much greater detail in chapter 6, this description of the French Socialists' economic policy is somewhat inaccurate, especially when we treat the policy mix of less government spending with a lower nominal interest rate as the more neoliberal policy mix. The 1983 U-turn did mark an important shift in the Socialist's policy mix, as they made inflation control a dominant economic policy objective. But the Socialist governments achieved lower inflation outcomes primarily through monetary, rather than fiscal, contraction. Indeed, French government consumption spending as a percent of GDP remained higher than the OECD average throughout the decade. Thus, the French Socialists moved toward the policy mix of more government spending with a higher nominal interest rate. This choice for domestic policy autonomy made exchange rate stability difficult to achieve, and the French government was forced to realign the franc within the EMS five times during the 1980s.

It seems clear that many leftist parties abandoned Keynesian ideas when they returned to power in certain advanced industrial democracies during the early 1990s. But this does not mean they adopted neoliberal ideas and accepted external policy convergence for exchange rate stability. As discussed in chapter

10. These last two examples were not discussed in McNamara's 1998 book, given her focus on events in Western Europe. On neoliberal policy ideas in the Japanese LDP, see Takenaka 1991, 129; Cargill, Hutchinson, and Ito 1997, 187.

2, new policy ideas had emerged by this time, ones that were more palatable to leftist interest groups and their ideological priorities than was monetarist economic theory. One very influential policy idea on the political left was endogenous growth—or new growth—theory (see Garrett and Lange 1991; Boix 1997, 1998). Much like Keynesian ideas, new growth strategies required government intervention in the national economy. But unlike Keynesian theory, which focused on demand-side intervention, new growth theory prescribed government intervention on the supply side. New growth theory held that government spending should be directed at public investment projects, notably those involving education, worker training, infrastructure, and research and development (see Aschauer 1990; Barro 1990; Romer 1990).

Perhaps supply-side fiscal expansion does not require such correspondingly high national interest rates and interest rate differentials as did demand-side fiscal expansion during the 1970s. But even government spending directed at the supply side of the national economy has demand-side implications. It can thus potentially increase inflationary expectations and raise prices in the national economy. For example, government spending on education and training boosts worker salaries, leading to greater private consumption and aggregate demand. Similarly, infrastructure projects employ large numbers of laborers, who use their wages largely for consumption purposes, rather than for investment. Consequently, increased government spending—even when it is directed at the supply side of the national economy—will require a higher interest rate for domestic price stability, thus translating into a larger national interest rate differential and greater exchange rate variability.

However, it is interesting to note that new growth theory says very little about the importance of exchange rate stability. Indeed, certain economists now question the link between fixed exchange rates, increased international trade, and a higher national income—both on an empirical basis (see, e.g., Edison and Melvin 1990; Levy-Yeyati and Sturzenegger 2003) and on a theoretical basis (see, e.g., Bacchetta and van Wincoop 2000). This is not to say that leftist governments have refused to make fixed exchange rate commitments in the post–Bretton Woods era. Many leftist governments joined the European Snake and, later, the exchange rate mechanism of the EMS. But both of these regimes were sufficiently flexible as to permit domestic policy autonomy, which such member states as France and Italy asserted to a very large degree (see Oatley 1997, chap. 5). Thus, reasoning from both opposing interest group pressures and different economic policy ideas, I expect to find partisan divergence with regard to the trade-off between domestic policy autonomy and exchange rate stability in the post–Bretton Woods era.

2. Political Power-Sharing

Scholars have recently focused their attention on how various electoral systems might influence national exchange rates. In one article in particular, Bernhard and Leblang (1999) showed that governments in high-opposition proportional representation (PR) electoral systems have been more likely to make formal fixed exchange rate commitments, perhaps to create a focal point for economic policy coordination. If one assumes that these fixed exchange rate commitments indicate greater external currency stability, then it would be natural to conclude that political power-sharing—the hallmark of PR regimes—leads national governments toward exchange rate stability and away from domestic policy autonomy.

This conclusion would seem to be strengthened by another article (Freeman, Hayes, and Stix 2000), which proposed that the consensual nature of PR electoral systems should help reduce the exchange rate variability resulting from political uncertainty. Comparing four bilateral exchange rates (between the United Kingdom and Ireland, the United States and Canada, Australia and New Zealand, and Germany and Sweden), the authors found that political factors had no effect on exchange rates in only the PR-PR dyad (Germany and Sweden). They thus concluded that other types of electoral systems "at worst exacerbate and at best do nothing to mitigate the effects of political (dis)equilibrium on currency markets" (ibid., 465).

Yet the empirical base for the conclusion that political power-sharing leads to exchange rate stability is somewhat thin. With regard to the second paper (Freeman, Hayes, and Stix 2000), the conclusion is largely based on the noneffect of political factors with regard to a single exchange rate between two PR political economies. Indeed, the conclusion might differ if one looked at the exchange rate outcomes of the many other advanced industrial democracies with PR electoral systems. With regard to Bernhard and Leblang's article (1999), I demonstrated in chapter 3 that commitments to OECD exchange rate regimes have been only weakly correlated with external currency stability in the post–Bretton Woods era. Thus, even if political power-sharing in PR systems leads coalition governments to make external monetary commitments, de jure fixed exchange rates will not translate into de facto exchange rate stability unless these governments also make domestic fiscal and monetary policy choices consistent with this external policy objective.

Given the empirical weakness of the proposition that political power-sharing leads to greater de facto exchange rate stability, I here consider a hypothesis in the opposite direction. My expectation is that political power-sharing will make exchange rate stability harder, not easier, to achieve. To develop this argument, I begin by considering the fiscal policy choice of democratic governments engaged in political power-sharing.

Perhaps the central problem facing power-sharing governments is how to maintain their diverse governing coalition and their position of political power. Indeed, it is not particularly heroic to assume that governments, once in power, wish to remain so. The trick for parties engaged in political power-sharing is to meet the economic needs of their own political base without jeopardizing the demands of other governing parties representing different economic constituencies. To this end, a power-sharing government should have a greater need to engage in targeted economic growth than would a single-party government. Power-sharing governments may also find it politically expedient to engage in income redistribution toward the various economic constituencies represented by the governing coalition, even when that governing coalition includes rightist parties who would normally be ideologically opposed to such transfers of wealth and income.

As described earlier in this chapter, fiscal expansion is much better suited for targeted economic growth and income redistribution than is monetary expansion. Thus, political power-sharing may lead governments to engage in greater spending because the alternative growth strategy—monetary expansion—is insufficient for targeting key supporters and achieving redistributive policy goals. Clark and Hallerberg (2000, 342) concluded: "although an increase in the money supply may help certain groups . . . more than others, it is a blunt instrument for cultivating specific clienteles. Fiscal policy, in contrast, is more suited to targeted use, whether through greater spending, tax cuts, or both." On this point, Roubini and Sachs (1989, 114) similarly concluded, "coalition governments will have a bias towards higher levels of government spending relative to majority party governments, as the various constituencies in the government undertake logrolling agreements to secure greater spending for their individual constituencies."

What does greater government spending on the part of power-sharing governments imply for national interest rates and exchange rate outcomes? According to the policy mix framework presented in chapter 4, if governments use their fiscal policy instrument to pursue targeted economic growth, they must reserve monetary policy as their instrument for inflation control with international capital mobility. This choice typically means a higher national interest rate and greater domestic monetary autonomy, as the national interest rate can be expected to move away from the nominally low world interest rate. This choice also suggests that power-sharing governments should be associated with greater exchange rate variability, despite any commitments that they might make to fix the value of the national currency.

The difficult experience of Italian governments within European monetary institutions suggests the plausibility of this hypothesis. Italian multiparty governments have traditionally held an expansionary fiscal policy, whether it is measured in terms of relative government spending, budget deficits, or even public debt. These facts suggest the "supremacy of fiscal policy over monetary policy" (Fratianni and Spinelli 1997, 212) for expanding the Italian economy. As the Italians assigned fiscal policy to the economic growth objective, monetary policy necessarily became the instrument for domestic price stability. As Posner (1978, 235) concluded early in the post–Bretton Woods era, Italian governments had to control domestic prices "largely by means of monetary policy," resulting in high Italian interest rates and interest rate differentials beginning in the mid-1970s.[11]

For the Italians, higher national interest rates were thus a deliberate policy choice to counterbalance greater government spending, especially since the Italian central bank has a relatively subordinate status, even after its so-called divorce in 1981.[12] The Italian governments' choice for domestic policy autonomy arguably contributed to the country's record number of realignments within the exchange rate mechanism of the EMS, despite the fact that Italy had wider bands (± 6 percent) than did the other member states (± 2.25 percent). Indeed, the cumulative currency adjustment for Italy was greater than that for any other EMS member state. Oatley (1997, 139) noted, "EMS flexibility granted the Italians a devaluation of about 7.5 percent approximately every six months and, thus, a fairly high degree of monetary autonomy."

While political power-sharing often occurs due to a PR electoral system, it can also emerge in countries with majoritarian electoral systems. Thus, a second example in which political power-sharing potentially made exchange rate stability harder to achieve occurred in the United States during the early 1980s, when the Republicans took power in the executive branch, with the Democrats holding substantial political power in the legislative branch. Such political power-sharing arguably contributed to the mix of loose fiscal and tight mone-

11. On the political infeasibility of fiscal contraction for inflation control, Posner (1978, 235) continued: "Italian fiscal policy 'is a resultant of bargaining among party factions. . . .' It is therefore caught up in the immobility of . . . coalition politics."

12. Consistent with the idea of deliberate monetary counterbalancing, Goodman (1992, 151–52) noted that when the Italian government asked the IMF for balance-of-payment financing in the early 1970s, the subordinate Bank of Italy raised interest rates well above the IMF's requirements: "Once the Italian government had approved the IMF program, the Banca d'Italia moved quickly to tighten monetary policy . . . adopt[ing] an economic program which was more restrictive than that suggested by the [IMF's] letter of intent."

tary policies held by the first Reagan administration. This policy mix is often cited as a key factor leading to the U.S. dollar's instability in an appreciating direction during the first half of the 1980s.[13]

We have just discussed how political power-sharing may push democratic governments away from exchange rate stability even when they may desire to achieve this external policy goal. It is now important to consider a countervailing factor, one that may help governments to reduce positive interest rate differentials and better achieve external monetary policy convergence for exchange rate stability. That factor is central bank independence.

3. Central Bank Independence

The argument that central bank independence can reduce interest rate differentials builds from a relatively well-established fact in economics literature. More independent central banks have been associated with lower inflation policy outcomes, at least for the advanced industrial economies (see Alesina and Summers 1993; Grilli, Masciandaro, and Tabellini 1991)—although the relationship does not hold for developing economies (see Cukierman, Webb, and Neyapti 1992) and less democratic polities (see Broz 2002). Central bank independence theoretically leads to lower inflation because more independent monetary authorities have greater freedom to increase national interest rates and contract the money supply when they see signs of rising domestic prices. Central banks that are subordinate to the government in power may be constrained from raising interest rates, since monetary contraction can reduce economic growth, undermining the government's reelection prospects. Superficially, this logic would seem to suggest that more independent central banks would be associated with higher nominal interest rates and more positive interest rate differentials.

This quick story, however, ignores the role of central bank credibility and its

---

13. Consistent with leftist preferences for domestic policy autonomy, it can also be argued that high U.S. interest rates during the first Reagan administration were largely a legacy of the Carter administration's autonomous policy choices. Sterling-Folker (2002, 158) wrote: "The seeds for potential exchange rate chaos had been sown before Ronald Reagan took office in January 1981. The expansionary [fiscal] policies adopted at the 1978 Bonn summit collided with the [monetary] contractions caused by the 1979 oil shock." Thus, the fact that the first Reagan administration could not stabilize the dollar at a more competitive level does not mean that certain parts of the administration were not interested in doing so. Such a reading of the evidence tends to confuse *ex post* policy outcomes with *ex ante* policy preferences. During the presidential campaign, several Reagan advisors had advocated a return to a Bretton Woods–style fixed exchange rate system (see Ferguson and Rogers 1986, 118; Grubaugh and Sumner 1990, 257) and inserted language into the 1980 Republican party platform concerning the "overriding objective of maintaining a stable dollar value" (see Stockman 1986, 63).

effect on national interest rates. If international capital markets view independent central banks as more credible in achieving lower inflation outcomes than their subordinate counterparts,[14] then independent monetary authorities may be able to hold lower interest rates—at least on a nominal basis—than subordinate central banks lacking such credibility. In other words, subordinate central banks must hold higher nominal interest rates to obtain the same amount of anti-inflation credibility as their independent counterparts.

This relationship between central bank independence and lower nominal interest rates does not mean that fiscal expansion will not lead to higher national interest rates as the central bank seeks to control inflation and reduce inflationary expectations (see fig. 11 in chap. 4). But it does suggest that at any given level of relative government spending, independent monetary authorities should be associated with lower rates and, thus, with lower interest rate differentials than subordinate central banks. If interest rate differentials can be reduced with more independent central banks, then this monetary commitment technology should also be associated with greater exchange rate stability, or reduced external currency variability.

This logic is potentially good news for both rightist and leftist governments. For rightist governments, the benefits of central bank independence are obvious. Independent central banks facilitate the rightist policy goals of external policy convergence with exchange rate stability, as discussed earlier in this chapter. Leftist governments tend to be more interested in the domestic benefits associated with increased government spending, but an independent central bank may allow them to achieve the necessary inflation control with lower corresponding nominal interest rates than could be achieved with a subordinate central bank. This possibility may help explain why leftist parties have supported moves to increase central bank independence since the early 1980s in several OECD countries, including Britain, France, Italy, Spain, Switzerland, and New Zealand.

4. Testing Hypotheses about Policy Divergence

The preceding theoretical discussion advanced a number of hypotheses concerning the relationship between the three independent variables of government partisanship, political power-sharing, and central bank independence, and the four different—but theoretically related—dependent variables of gov-

14. For a concise statement on the credibility of independent central banks, see Bernhard, Broz, and Clark 2002.

ernment spending, nominal interest rates, domestic monetary autonomy, and exchange rate variability. These hypotheses are concisely summarized in table 4. Leftist governments are expected to be associated with more government spending relative to GDP and higher nominal interest rates. Given this fiscal and monetary policy stance in the post–Bretton Woods era, leftist governments are also expected to be associated with greater domestic monetary policy autonomy and increased exchange rate variability.

A similar set of relationships is hypothesized for political power-sharing. Such power-sharing is expected to lead governments toward greater relative government spending, higher nominal interest rates, greater domestic monetary policy autonomy, and increased exchange rate variability. Conversely, central bank independence is expected to lower nominal interest rates in the domestic economy, thereby reducing the interest rate differential (the operational measure for domestic monetary policy autonomy) and exchange rate variability.

These hypotheses are tested on the same panel of twenty-three OECD countries that was examined in chapters 3 and 4. The temporal coverage is slightly reduced (1975–97), due to data limitations that will be discussed shortly; hence, $N = 529$. With four different dependent variables, I estimate four separate models, each of which takes the general form of equation (5.1).[15]

TABLE 4. Hypothesized Relationships between Domestic Political Factors and National Policy Instruments and Exchange Rate Variability

	Government spending/GDP	Nominal interest rates	Domestic monetary policy autonomy	Exchange rate variability
Leftist governments	+	+	+	+
Political power-sharing	+	+	+	+
Central bank independence	−	−	−	−

15. I used a common right-hand specification for these four models for theoretical reasons. As I argued in chapter 4, governments and their national monetary authorities choose a policy mix based on a common set of dominant policy goals. Thus, I needed to control for the same set of factors in each equation. Another reason I used a common specification was to avoid giving any readers the impression that my results for a particular model are due to an idiosyncratic model specification. In fact, the results of interest are robust with regard to other possible control variables, including unemployment, various trade measures, and different measures of de jure exchange rate regimes; for other model specifications, see Bearce 2003. Since the models presented in the current study include a full set of country- and year-specific fixed effects, concerns about omitted variable bias are greatly reduced.

$$DV_{it} = \beta_0 + \beta_1 {}^*GDPGROWTH_{it} + \beta_2 {}^*INFLATION_{it} + \beta_3 {}^*GDPPC_{it}$$
$$+ \beta_4 {}^*KOPEN_{it} + \beta_5 {}^*LEFTGOV_{it} + \beta_6 {}^*SHARE_{it} + \beta_7 {}^*CBI_{it}$$
$$+ \alpha_i {}^*COUNTRY_i + \alpha_t {}^*YEAR_t + e_{it} \qquad (5.1)$$

In equation (5.1), DV represents one of four dependent variables. The first is GOVCON, which measures the current level of government consumption expenditures as a percent of country i's GDP in year t.[16] The second dependent variable is INTRATE, which measures country i's policy interest rate in year t. This variable was introduced in chapter 4, where a more comprehensive discussion of its construction and validity is provided. The third dependent variable is MONAUT, introduced in chapter 3. This variable captures the extent of domestic monetary policy autonomy in terms of country i's nominal interest rate differential relative to the prevailing external interest rate in year t. Finally, the fourth dependent variable is EXRCV, also introduced in chapter 3. This variable measures the coefficient of nominal variation for country i's national currency versus the SDR in year t. Higher (or lower) values indicate more (or less) exchange rate variability.

Equation (5.1) includes seven independent variables in addition to the country- and year-specific fixed effects. Considering that all governments can be expected to make some adjustments to monetary and fiscal policy in response to economic growth and inflation, I included the variables GDPGROWTH and INFLATION as controls.[17] As shown in chapter 4, the level of economic development affects the national interest rate and possibly other related policy decisions as well, so I also included the per capita level of country i's GDP in year t (GDPPC).[18] The last economic control variable I included in this model is KOPEN, introduced in chapter 3. This variable measures country i's financial openness in year t, updating the data from Quinn and Inclan (1997).

The remaining three independent variables in the model were included to test the various hypotheses specified in table 4. LEFTGOV measures the partisan character of the government in power for country i in year t, using a common five-point scale. LEFTGOV is coded as 4 for a left-dominant government, 3 for a left-center government, 2 for a balanced government, 1 for a right-center government, and 0 for a right-dominant government.[19] SHARE measures

16. As discussed in chapter 4, government consumption is arguably the most valid way to capture a government's discretionary spending decisions. Total government spending includes other categories of expenditures, including interest payments, which are essentially obligatory in character. The data are provided by the OECD in *Annual National Accounts* (1975–97).

17. The data come from the World Bank's *World Development Indicators* (1975–97).

18. The data come from the World Bank's *World Development Indicators* (1975–97).

19. The data come from Woldendorp, Keman, and Budge 1993. I used their coding rules and data from Lane, McCay, and Newton 1997 to fill in the missing country panels.

the extent of political power-sharing for country i in year t, using a measure of government party fractionalization. This variable is continuous between 0 and 1, with higher values indicating greater power-sharing among different political parties.[20] Finally, CBI measures the independence of state i's central bank in year t. This variable is also continuous between 0 and 1, with higher values indicating greater central bank independence from the government in power. Following Bernhard (1998), this measure uses a normalized mean score from three different sources (Alesina and Summers 1993; Cukierman, Webb, and Neyapti 1992; Grilli, Masciandro, and Tabellini 1991) to minimize the effect of coding disagreements.

The estimates for the four models are reported together in table 5. Of the eleven hypotheses summarized in table 4, eight receive statistical support, and three do not. The strongest results clearly emerged for the government partisanship variable (LEFTGOV), which is statistically significant with a positive sign in all four models. That leftist governments are associated with more government consumption spending and higher interest rates is consistent with Garrett's results (1995, 1998b), but the analysis here goes much further. The results in columns 3 and 4 also show how this policy mix moved leftist governments toward greater domestic monetary policy autonomy and exchange rate variability. While additional results are not reported here for space considerations, leftist governments were also associated with greater exchange rate variability when national currency instability was measured relative to the German mark and the U.S. dollar.[21]

Political power-sharing is also significantly associated with more government consumption spending. The SHARE variable is not, however, associated with higher interest rates or larger interest rate differentials. One possible explanation is that certain parties within the governing coalition—notably those on the political right preferring monetary over fiscal expansion—

20. The data come from the World Bank's "Database of Political Institutions" (Beck et al. 2001). The data coverage begins in 1975, thus restricting the temporal domain of my pooled time-series models in this chapter to the 1975–97 period. As discussed earlier, power-sharing has a different meaning depending on a country's electoral institution. For countries with high-opposition PR electoral systems (Germany, Italy, Netherlands, Belgium, Denmark, Austria, Sweden, Finland, Norway, and Switzerland), where power-sharing focuses on executive branch divisions, I used the World Bank's measure GOVFRAC. For countries with low-opposition PR electoral systems (Greece, Ireland, Spain, and Portugal) and majoritarian electoral systems (the United States, Japan, Britain, France, Canada, Australia, New Zealand, and Turkey), where power-sharing extends into the legislative branch, I used the World Bank's measure FRAC. On the importance of distinguishing between high- and low-opposition PR electoral systems, see Bernhard and Leblang 1999, 77.

21. For results showing leftist governments associated with greater exchange rate variability versus the German mark, see Bearce 2003, 406. Results showing that leftist governments are associated with greater variability versus the U.S. dollar are available from the author on request.

demanded lower interest rates as their part of the coalition's economic policy compromise. Another possibility is that many advanced industrial democracies with a long history of power-sharing governments have made their central banks more independent (Bernhard 1998, 2002). This fact should help reduce nominal interest rates and interest rate differentials, thus offsetting some of the contrary pressures associated with more government spending. But even so, political power-sharing is significantly associated with greater external currency variability, or exchange rate instability, as hypothesized earlier.

Also as hypothesized, more independent central banks are strongly associated with both lower nominal interest rates and smaller interest rate differentials. Central bank independence is not, however, significantly associated with a corresponding reduction in exchange rate variability. This weak result could emerge if central bank independence also leads governments to engage in greater government spending, a policy choice that is largely inconsistent with more stable exchange rates.[22] Indeed, the result in the first column suggests a

TABLE 5.   **Estimates of Domestic Political Factors on National Policy Instruments and Exchange Rate Variability**

Dependent variable	1 GOVCON	2 INTRATE	3 MONAUT	4 EXRCV
Constant	16.28***	23.44***	14.01**	2.14
	(1.71)	(6.62)	(6.17)	(2.93)
GDPGROWTH	−0.07***	−0.06	−0.10	−0.05
	(0.01)	(0.11)	(0.11)	(0.05)
INFLATION	−0.04***	0.23**	0.21**	0.14***
	(0.01)	(0.09)	(0.09)	(0.03)
GDPPC	−0.00009***	−0.00056***	−0.00046***	−0.00004
	(0.00002)	(0.00016)	(0.00014)	(0.00004)
KOPEN	0.03	0.65***	0.77***	0.20**
	(0.04)	(0.21)	(0.21)	(0.09)
LEFTGOV	0.053**	0.37**	0.34**	0.14**
	(0.027)	(0.16)	(0.16)	(0.06)
SHARE	0.47*	−0.27	−0.65	1.33*
	(0.25)	(1.66)	(1.69)	(0.76)
CBI	2.52	−26.02***	−23.66***	−5.73
	(2.03)	(7.76)	(7.58)	(3.94)
N	529	529	529	529
R^2	0.97	0.76	0.63	0.76

Note: Estimates are Prais-Winsten coefficients, including an AR1 correction, with panel-corrected standard errors in parentheses. Individual country and year dummies are not reported.

Two-tailed statistical significance is indicated as follows: ***$p < .01$, **$p < .05$, *$p < .10$.

22. For a more developed explanation of this result, see Bearce 2005.

weak, but positive, relationship between greater central bank independence and more government spending.[23]

Beyond evaluating the main hypotheses for the domestic political factors, it is also important to consider how some of the economic control variables affect the policy mix and the resultant trade-off between domestic monetary autonomy and exchange rate stability. More developed capitalist economies (i.e., those with a larger GDPPC) naturally spend less on a relative basis and have lower nominal interest rates. Together, these results show that if governments are going to move toward the fiscal and monetary policies of the most developed states in the international system (i.e., external policy convergence), they must move toward the policy mix of less government spending with a lower nominal interest rate for reduced domestic monetary policy autonomy and exchange rate variability (see fig. 14 in chap. 4).

But such external policy convergence is harder, not easier, to achieve with international capital mobility. Larger values of KOPEN are associated with more government consumption spending[24] and higher nominal interest rates. These facts suggest that international capital mobility should also be associated with more domestic monetary policy autonomy and increased exchange rate variability. Indeed, these results are statistically significant in the third and fourth columns of table 5. Thus, international capital mobility does not lead OECD governments toward a more externally convergence policy stance. To the contrary, it appears to make external policy convergence harder to achieve, a result consistent with the proposition of macroeconomic policy divergence in the post–Bretton Woods era.

5. Toward a New Theory of Partisan Politics in the Post–Bretton Woods Era

The policy mix framework presented in chapter 4 and the government partisanship results presented in this chapter lead toward a new theory of partisan economic policy-making with international capital mobility. This point may not be obvious to many readers, so it is useful to compare the partisan policy mix framework with two other partisan theories. Table 6 summarizes their differing convergence and divergence predictions in terms of both economic policy goals and policy instruments.

23. Other model specifications produce a statistically significant positive result; see, for example, Bearce 2002, 213.

24. The result is not quite statistically significant in this model specification. For a model specification with a statistically significant result, see Bearce 2002, 213.

The traditional partisan-ideological thesis has several variations (see, e.g., Kirschen et al. 1964; Hibbs 1977; Alt 1985; Garrett 1995, 1998b; Oatley 1999). But in the broadest sense, traditional partisan theories argue for partisan divergence in terms of both dominant economic policy goals and the policy instruments used to achieve these goals. In terms of policy goals, leftist parties are expected to have stronger preferences for economic growth and fuller employment, caring somewhat less about domestic inflation. Conversely, rightist parties have stronger preferences for low inflation outcomes, with much weaker preferences for economic growth to increase employment.

Traditional partisan arguments were largely tested on economic policy outcomes, not on the use of policy instruments.[25] But the partisan-ideological thesis generally theorized that leftist governments would use all available policy instruments, both fiscal and monetary, to achieve economic growth with fuller employment.[26] Since inflation control was only a minor concern, no policy instrument needed to be reserved for this economic objective. Leftist governments were theoretically expected to move toward a policy mix defined by more government spending and lower interest rates (Garrett 1995, 670). Conversely, rightist governments were expected to move in the opposite direction (toward less government spending with a higher interest rate), with both policy instruments generally directed toward domestic price stability.

Perhaps such strong partisan divergence, in terms of both policy goals and policy instruments, was possible during the period of restricted international capital mobility after World War II. But this story becomes harder to defend

TABLE 6.   Three Theories of Partisan Economic Policy Goals and Instruments

Theory	Prediction about policy goals	Prediction about policy instruments
Traditional partisan- ideological thesis	*Divergence*	*Divergence*
Macroeconomic convergence hypothesis	*Convergence*	*Convergence*
Partisan policy mix framework	*Convergence*	*Divergence*

25. For important exceptions, see Garrett 1995; Garrett 1998b, chap. 4; Oatley 1999.

26. Oatley (1999) amended the traditional partisan argument to fit open-economy models, where governments have only one effective policy instrument—either fiscal policy with fixed exchange rates or monetary policy with floating exchange rates.

with the financial market integration that began to reemerge at the end of the Bretton Woods system and that exploded in the post–Bretton Woods era. Much like the macroeconomic convergence hypothesis advanced in the early 1990s, the partisan policy mix framework presented here takes seriously the idea that international capital mobility constrains the economic policy goals of national governments. But unlike the macroeconomic convergence hypothesis, which focused almost exclusively on the need for governments to maintain low inflation, the policy mix framework also recognizes the need for governments to maintain a growing national economy. This means that partisan governments have been constrained to make inflation control and economic growth their two dominant macroeconomic policy objectives. The political left has certainly taken inflation control more seriously in the post–Bretton Woods era, but the political right has also learned the importance of sustained growth and the need to avoid economic recessions.[27]

This logic about how international capital mobility constrains certain domestic economic policy goals accords with Clark's evidence (2003, chap. 5) that there are relatively few strong partisan differences with regard to such macroeconomic outcomes as GDP growth, actual inflation, and unemployment, although Clark used a different theoretical logic to get to these results.[28] But partisan convergence in terms of such economic policy goals does not mean that there should also be convergence in the use of policy instruments, as scholars advancing the macroeconomic convergence hypothesis have tended to assume.

With regard to the capital mobility constraint, Mosley (2000, 766) interviewed financial market participants and concluded: "provided governments achieve the desired outcomes, market actors do not worry about which means is employed. These choices . . . are well within the purview of domestic politics." With regard to Downsian theories of partisan convergence toward the median voter (see Downs 1957), while the median voter likely cares about such economic outcomes as growth and inflation, it is not at all clear that the median voter should care about the policy instruments used to reach these outcomes, provided that the preferred outcome is indeed achieved. Quinn and Shapiro (1991, 659) wrote: "one strong objection to the necessity of conver-

27. On how rightist economic policies have often permitted—even engineered—economic recessions during the Bretton Woods system, see Alesina and Rosenthal 1995, 180–81.

28. To the extent that we observe some limited partisan divergence in terms of these economic outcomes, it may have to do more with the effectiveness of the different policy mixes used by partisan governments than with different partisan economic policy objectives, or goals, in the post–Bretton Woods era.

gence to a mean among parties is that different strategies can yield similar rates of economic growth, thereby satisfying the convergent policy goal."

Thus, partisan divergence in the use of policy instruments remains theoretically possible. But such partisan divergence should not take the form specified by traditional partisan-ideological theories. The Old Left policy mix, defined by more government spending with a lower nominal interest rate, is no longer feasible in the post–Bretton Woods era, as discussed in chapter 4. The results in the present chapter show how leftist governments have instead shifted toward a policy mix marked by more government spending with a higher nominal interest rate (see fig. 16). Likewise, the Old Right policy mix, with two policy instruments dedicated to inflation control, is no longer feasible with international capital mobility. To accommodate the need for low inflation with economic growth, rightist governments have effectively moved toward a policy mix defined by less government spending with a lower nominal interest rate. This New Right policy mix was labeled as the neoliberal alternative in chapter 4.

While Garrett's work hinted at these new partisan policy mixes in the post–Bretton Woods era, the analysis here goes at least two steps further. First, it provides a model explicitly linking domestic fiscal and monetary policy choices, developing the logic of deliberate monetary counterbalancing in response to increased government spending.[29] This allows scholars to do more in the examination of the use of policy instruments than just test compensation versus efficiency hypotheses (see Garrett 1995, 671). The policy mix framework explains why partisan governments must be concerned about both compensation and economic efficiency but that differences with regard to who they compensate and how they obtain their economic efficiency should produce partisan divergence concerning government spending and nominal interest rates. Second, this analysis shows how partisan divergence in the use of such policy instruments has clear and important implications for the trade-off between domestic policy autonomy and exchange rate stability in the post–Bretton Woods era, a topic not considered in Garrett's study of partisan politics with economic globalization.

The results in this chapter have demonstrated that we can find statistically significant partisan differences precisely where the partisan policy mix framework expected to find them—in terms of government consumption spending, nominal interest rates, interest rate differentials, and exchange rate variability. But can this evidence of partisan policy divergence be squared with Clark's conclusion (2003, chap. 3) that just as there are no meaningful partisan differences concerning economic policy outcomes, there are also no significant par-

---

29. Garrett (1998b, 102) seemingly rejected the idea of deliberate monetary counterbalancing.

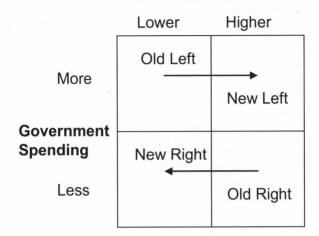

Fig. 16.   Partisan Policy Mix Divergence

tisan differences concerning the use of fiscal and monetary instruments? I believe this is possible, because Clark, in fact, found some evidence of partisan divergence concerning the use of fiscal and monetary policy instruments.

With regard to fiscal policy, he reported some significant partisan differences in terms of government consumption but fewer such differences with regard to income transfers, total spending, and budget deficits. This set of results is not particularly surprising, since of the various possible spending measures, government consumption best captures the discretionary fiscal policy choices made by current governments. On this point, income transfer spending is effectively obligatory in character, being known as the so-called third rail in U.S. domestic politics, since any politician trying to cut such spending is likely to find his or her political life cut short. Partisan governments are not easily able to change this category of government spending, especially from year-to-year, the time frame investigated here. The same is true for total government spending, since it includes yet another category of obligatory expenditures, that of interest payments on debt. Interest payments largely reflect the spending decisions made by previous governments and then imposed on the current government. While total government spending includes discretionary consumption expenditures, the obligatory categories effectively add noise to the signal of a government's fiscal policy intentions, making expected relationships much harder to find in the data.

The lack of partisan differences with regard to budget deficits is also not problematic for the partisan divergence argument advanced here. Since leftist governments tend to balance greater discretionary spending with more tax revenues (Garrett 1995, 674; Garrett 1998b, 90; Cusack 1999; Clark 2003, 66–67), we should not expect to see significant partisan differences with regard to either budget deficits or public debt. But these results do not mean that there are not important partisan differences concerning fiscal policy instruments. Although it may produce similar outcomes with regard to deficits and debt, the strategy of more spending with higher taxes has markedly different macroeconomic implications than the strategy defined by less spending with lower taxes.

On this point, Clark (2003, 70–72, 78, 81) also reported some significant partisan differences with regard to national interest rates, with leftist governments associated with high interest rates, much like they are in the results reported here. For Clark, this finding was problematic because it ran contrary to the expectations of traditional partisan-ideological theories, which posited the political left as more expansionary in terms of its monetary policy choices. But this result is not at all problematic for the policy mix framework, which expects the Left to hold higher interest rates to counterbalance its choice for greater government spending.

In short, what Clark (2003) viewed as only minor partisan fiscal and monetary policy divergence is identified as a major difference by the partisan policy mix framework. Policy divergence in terms of government consumption spending and nominal interest rates represents a major difference because it has important implications for the trade-off between domestic monetary autonomy and exchange rate stability, as the statistical results in this chapter demonstrate. Chapter 6 will further illustrate this partisan policy divergence, presenting contrasting case studies on the French Socialists and British Conservatives.

CHAPTER 6

Illustrating Partisan Divergence in the Policy Mix

Chapter 5 provided large-N statistical evidence concerning the determinants of policy divergence among the OECD governments in the post–Bretton Woods era. These quantitative results showed how the partisan character of the government in power played an important role at least with regard to government spending and nominal interest rates, with related consequences for domestic monetary autonomy and exchange rate stability. Leftist governments were significantly associated with more government spending, higher nominal interest rates, larger interest rate differentials, and greater exchange rate variability than were their rightist counterparts.

This chapter will further develop these partisan results by presenting two detailed case examples to illustrate partisan policy mix divergence in the post–Bretton Woods era. Indeed, scholars have a right to be suspicious of statistical evidence that cannot be illustrated and supported by interesting and important case examples. The first such case example will be the French Socialists, who governed their national economy for most of the period from 1981 to 1995. The British Conservatives will be the second case example, having decided the direction of their national economy from 1979 to 1996.

The examples of the French Socialists and British Conservatives are already well-studied cases in comparative and international political economy, but I wish to revisit them here based on the belief that both cases have been somewhat misinterpreted with regard to the hypothesis of macroeconomic policy convergence after 1973. The convergence hypothesis predicted that the OECD governments were moving toward very similar fiscal and monetary policy strategies for governing their national economies with international capital mobility. To the extent that the convergence hypothesis allowed for variation in the extent and timing of national policy convergence, the governments within fixed exchange rate regimes such as the EMS were expected to be the most policy convergent; those outside such regimes were expected to be somewhat less so but nonetheless still on a similar trajectory toward external policy convergence.

Following this conventional wisdom, one might identify the French Socialists, with their formal commitment to the exchange rate mechanism (ERM) of the EMS, as a powerful example of external policy convergence, especially after President Mitterrand's so-called U-turn in 1983. Indeed, as was discussed in chapter 5, scholars have often treated the French Socialists as a crucial case for the partisan economic policy convergence argument, since France was the only G-7 economy governed by a leftist party for a substantial part of the 1980s, a critical time period for the macroeconomic policy convergence hypothesis.

Britain represents a more awkward case for convergence theory, because the Conservative governments generally stayed outside European monetary and exchange rate institutions, a fact thought to suggest policy nonconvergence. Yet the Conservatives also followed neoliberal policy ideas, a fact consistent with certain explanations for monetary policy convergence (see, e.g., McNamara 1998). Thus, Conservative Party governance in Britain could still be consistent with external policy convergence, but the conventional wisdom would read the British Conservatives as a laggard case and, thus, as somewhat less convergent than the French Socialists, who remained within the EMS throughout the two Mitterrand presidencies.

Having argued in the earlier chapters that we cannot judge domestic policy autonomy or external policy convergence in terms of a government's de jure exchange rate regime, I will now make the case that the conventional wisdom has misidentified these two important case examples (see fig. 17). Rather than being more convergent as identified by the macroeconomic convergence hypothesis, the French Socialists are an important example of policy autonomy and nonconvergence in the post–Bretton Woods era, consistent with the argument made in chapter 5 that leftist governments have tended to choose domestic policy independence over exchange rate stability and that they have been able to make this choice even inside such exchange rate regimes as the EMS. Likewise, I will argue that rather than being somewhat less convergent (or a laggard case of policy convergence) due to their nonmembership in European exchange rate regimes, the British Conservatives are, in fact, a much better example of external policy convergence than the French Socialists. With these two cases, I can illustrate partisan policy divergence in terms of government spending, nominal interest rates, and exchange rate variability. The remainder of this chapter will present these two cases, looking at the French Socialists first and at the British Conservatives second.

	French Socialists	British Conservatives
Macroeconomic convergence hypothesis	More convergent since inside the EMS	Less convergent since outside the EMS
Partisan policy mix divergence	Less convergent with policy autonomy inside the EMS	More convergent despite the lack of EMS commitments

Fig. 17.   Identifying the French and British Cases

1.   The French Socialists, 1981–95

For scholars seeking historical support for the macroeconomic convergence hypothesis, Socialist Party governments in France are often cited as the prime example of the political left adopting rightist policies for managing the national economy. Two facts would seem to bear out this conclusion. The first is President Mitterrand's so-called U-turn in 1983, when he decided to keep France within the exchange rate mechanism of the EMS. The second is Mitterrand's later support for the Economic and Monetary Union (EMU) in Europe. These decisions might suggest that the Socialist Party moved the French economy toward external policy convergence and exchange rate stability in the post–Bretton Woods era.

However, when placed in a broader context, this conclusion seems not only misleading but factually incorrect. The 1983 U-turn did represent an important shift in the Socialists' policy mix, as the leftist party accepted the need for low inflation to become a dominant economic policy objective. But Socialist governments achieved their lower inflation outcomes primarily through monetary, not fiscal, contraction. While government spending might have been reduced relative to planned expenditure levels, French government consumption as a percent of GDP remained higher than the OECD average throughout the Mitterrand presidencies. Thus, the French Socialists did not follow the neoliberal policy mix of less government spending with a lower nominal interest rate that is associated with external policy convergence for exchange rate stability. Instead, the Socialists shifted toward the New Left combination of more government spending with a higher nominal interest rate to better achieve their partisan goals of redistribution and public goods provision. As described earlier, this was not a policy mix associated with external monetary convergence; consequently, the Socialists paid some costs in terms of greater exchange rate variability.

Certainly, Mitterrand kept France within the EMS, but this decision reflected his personal commitment to European institutions, rather than the Socialist Party's collective preference for exchange rate stability over domestic policy autonomy. Indeed, despite the built-in flexibility offered by this exchange rate regime (with currency bands that allowed national currencies to float freely within a 4.5 percent range before any intervention was required), the Socialists realigned the franc within the EMS six times during the Mitterrand era (in October 1981, June 1982, March 1983, July 1985, April 1986, and September 1992).[1] Inasmuch as Mitterrand still felt restricted within the German-dominated EMS, he proposed and supported a new European arrangement designed to restore French monetary independence. Paradoxically, Mitterrand's support for the EMU—which was not shared by many other Socialist Party leaders—was based on the mistaken belief that the new European monetary regime would offer France greater policy flexibility, especially vis-à-vis Germany. The rest of this case study will develop these arguments in greater detail.

The Socialist's Societal Base

Like many leftist parties in the advanced industrial democracies, the French Socialists tended to represent domestically oriented producer groups, those with expected preferences for domestic policy autonomy over exchange rate stability. The Socialists have certainly competed with the Communist Parties in France for support from low-skilled labor and traditional manufacturing. This competition suggests that the Socialists should be particularly attentive to the policy preferences of the "import-competing producers of tradable goods for the domestic market" (Frieden 1991, 445).

The French Socialists have also sought political support from the growing service sector, especially those working in public and government services (i.e., "producers of nontradable goods and services" [ibid.]). Bell and Criddle (1988,

---

1. For more details on the French EMS realignments, see Ungerer 1997, 174.

208) concluded: "Advancing more on the votes of the expanding new middle class than on the contracting industrial working class, and internally dominated by the new professionals in teaching and administration, the PS is the Party of the tertiary (largely public) sector, credentialed (not propertied) middle class. . . . Popular (in 1981) with the working class, it lacks deep roots in that class. Capable also of taking 'protest' votes from the parties of the Right, it cannot rely on such support." Cole (1994, 66–67) provided further evidence that these domestically oriented economic sectors tend to support leftist parties in France, identifying the Socialists as an "interclassist" party, which "attracted support from many of the new social groups produced by post-war socio-economic and demographic change: new tertiary sector workers (especially in the public sector), the new and expanded professions (teaching, social work), as well as a high proportion of the cadres, the managerial strata whose ranks had increased dramatically in the post-war period." Cole continued: "In addition to these dynamic expanding groups within French society, the party proved remarkably successful at attracting the support of older, more traditionally left-wing constituencies, such as industrial workers, and low status office and shop-workers (employés), over which the Communist Party had traditionally exercised a strong influence."

As the Socialists obtained their greatest political support from import-competing manufacturing and nontradable services, the party could be expected to face strong interest group pressure for domestic policy autonomy. Indeed, for societal groups wishing to obtain their economic policy preferences, partisan agents have become a necessity in the French political system. Scholars typically treat the French state, especially with regard to economic policy-making, as quite strong relative to French society, making it difficult for interest groups to influence policy directly and forcing them to employ political agents for this purpose. Unions, as potential agents for influencing the French state, tend to be weak. Hayward (1986, 53) noted, "in reality these [French] union have had to confine their inordinate ambitions to acting rather negatively, resisting policies that they disliked rather than promoting policies which they desire." To influence positively the French state on economic matters, societal actors instead rely on "the mediation of political parties" (ibid., 48). Hayward thus concluded: "while the political party [in the Fifth Republic] does not play the monopoly role that it enjoys in the one-party state and parties pursue less divergent policies when in power than would be expected from their ideologies or programmes in opposition, it continues to have an important place among the plurality of political actors in France" (54).

Predictably, Francois Mitterrand, as the Socialist Party's presidential candidate, ran in 1981 on a platform of French policy independence. Howarth (2001, 80) summarized: "The policies of the Socialist Party prior to the 1981 elections and the rhetoric of its leadership created considerable expectation within the Party's rank and file, the new government and the trade unions of the pursuit of social and economic policies which would transform French society. This expectation increased opposition to the ERM [of the EMS], as the most obvious manifestation of the 'international capitalist' constraint which prevented the fulfillment of Socialist goals. Much of Mitterrand's rhetorical commitment to growth-oriented policies, under-emphasis of austerity, and his statements suggesting the possibility of a franc devaluation outside the ERM stemmed from the need to mollify this demand." The previous right-centrist government led by Valery Giscard d'Estaing—representing capital-intensive internationally oriented producer groups (see Bell and Criddle 1988; Hayward 1986) with much stronger preferences for stable exchange rates—was instrumental in constructing the EMS and initially committed France to this multilateral exchange rate regime. Although the Socialists did not directly repudiate French EMS membership, they expressed little genuine interest in exchange rate stability. Goodman (1992, 127) argued: "Most Socialist party leaders agreed on these points [economic expansion with redistribution], but far less accord existed on the question of exchange rate policy. Although Mitterrand's electoral policy promised to defend the franc, it was never clear how this goal would be reconciled with the government's commitment to domestic growth. One leading Socialist economist admitted: 'We were thinking more about growth, protecting employment, and structural reforms. . . . Defending the franc was a secondary consideration.'"

Upon Mitterrand's victory in the 1981 presidential elections, the Socialists obtained their first opportunity to govern the French economy in the post–Bretton Woods era. This fact is important because it suggests that they had little experience with economic governance given the constraints imposed by international capital mobility. Inheriting a situation of rising unemployment and slow domestic growth, Mitterrand began with an Old Left reflation policy, described as "redistributive Keynesianism" (Hall 1986, 194), using relatively loose fiscal and monetary policies. Mitterrand's reflation program had three main components: increase the minimum wage to boost private consumption, increase welfare benefits, and boost economic growth with greater government spending, including worker training and funding for research and development (see Muet and Fonteneau 1990, 75). Goodman (1992, 127) wrote: "In the Socialists' macroeconomic strategy, fiscal policy became the principal motor of economic growth. In fact, little attention was paid to monetary policy, which was expected to accommodate [i.e., remain loose to facilitate] the planned increase in government spending."

But as the policy mix framework predicted, Mitterand's Old Left policy mix (high government spending and low national interest rates) would quickly become unsustainable with international capital mobility, since no policy instrument was directed toward inflation control. Indeed, the French economic situation worsened as inflation rose and the twin deficits (budget and trade) grew. Mobile capital exercised its exit option, and the French franc lost value. The declining economy forced President Mitterrand to consider a shift in the French policy mix. But his party was internally divided on how best to proceed.

On one side stood the CERES group (members of the Centre d'Etudes de Recherche et d'Education Socialistes), led by Jean-Pierre Chevenment, who wanted to pursue full economic expansion regardless of the inflationary consequences, withdraw from the EMS, and institute trade and capital controls to buffer against external pressures. Capital controls, to the extent that they could be maintained, would make the Old Left policy mix a more feasible policy option. The so-called Second Left (*deuxieme gauche*) opposed this plan. Michel Rocard and Jacques Delors, the latter of whom served as the Socialist finance minister at the time, argued for monetary contraction to restore domestic price stability, while remaining open to the world economy. The Second Left argued that continued EMS membership could provide some anti-inflation credibility even if exchange rate stability was not an important Socialist economic priority (Oatley 1997, 111–20).

U-turn or "New Left" Turn?

The Second Left gradually won this policy struggle, as France undertook a series of austerity programs and realignments inside the EMS. In late 1981, the Mitterrand government began to raise nominal interest rates in the French national economy. Higher interest rates reflected a deliberate policy choice on the part of the Socialist-led government, since the French central bank, the Banque de France, was quite subordinate to the Socialist finance ministry in setting monetary policy. As shown in figure 18, French nominal interest rate differentials remained positive (above the prevailing world interest rate) throughout the fourteen years of the two Mitterrand presidencies, reflecting domestic monetary policy autonomy in an international context. Figure 18 also shows that during the cohabitation years (particularly 1987–88 and 1993–94) when Gaullist ministers ran French economic policy under a Mitter-

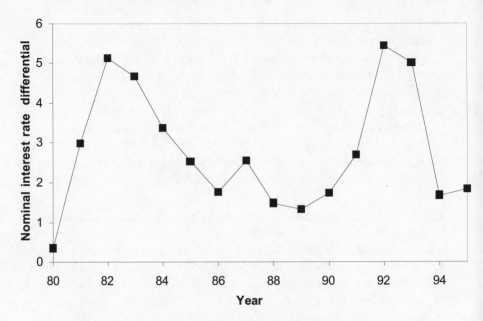

Fig. 18.   French Monetary Policy Autonomy, 1980–95. (Monetary policy data
from International Monetary Fund, *International Financial Statistics.*)

rand presidency, French interest rate differentials tended to decline, consistent
with rightist preferences for external monetary convergence toward the low
world interest rate.

The tight money policy instituted by the Socialists beginning in 1981 took
some time to reduce inflation. During this period, the lack of external monetary policy convergence in France predictably led to exchange rate instability.
France realigned within the EMS first in October 1981, again in June 1982, and
a third time in March 1983. In 1983, Delors, as finance minister, instituted an
even tighter monetary policy, as measured in terms of money supply growth.
Goodman (1992, 135) reported: "An implicit target for the growth of domestic
credit was set at 12 percent, a significant drop from the previous year. But
Delors reportedly rejected the central bank's proposal and set a 10 percent target, apparently anticipating that the government would have to tighten monetary policy even further in 1983."

Socialist monetary tightness eventually produced the desired effect in stabilizing domestic prices. Loriaux (1991, 220) argued: "The Socialist party out-
performed its conservative predecessor in its efforts to impose price stability
and to contain the growth of wages. By 1985, the Socialists had brought

inflation to under 6 percent, compared with an average in excess of 10 percent under the government of Raymond Barre [Giscard's prime minister]." But despite such low inflation outcomes, the Socialist monetary policy never converged on the low world interest rate, as shown in figure 18. This evidence accords well with the data presented by Bilger (1993, 111, 114) showing that French interest rates and inflation rates never fully converged on those in West Germany during the 1980s.

Such monetary nonconvergence can be explained in large part by the Socialists' expansionary fiscal policy stance over this period. At the same time that the Socialist government directed its monetary policy instrument toward inflation control, it needed another policy instrument to help maintain economic growth, consistent with the logic of the policy mix framework. Given Socialist ideological objectives favoring public goods and income redistribution, their preferred policy instrument for economic growth was fiscal expansion.

Certainly, Mitterrand began his tenure in 1981 with an expansionary fiscal stance. But it is often argued that the two austerity programs, the first coming in June 1982 and the second in March 1983, led to drastic cuts in French government spending. The empirical evidence simply does not bear out such a conclusion. As figure 19 demonstrates, contrary to the conventional wisdom, French government consumption relative to GDP actually grew during the austerity years (1982–83). As compared to the OECD average, French fiscal policy was relatively expansionary throughout the two Mitterrand presidencies (1981–95). Also consistent with the partisan policy mix framework, French government spending tended to contract when the Right controlled fiscal policy instruments during the cohabitation years (1986–88 and 1993–95).

How can it be that the Socialists' fiscal policy—at least as measured in terms of relative government consumption spending—was relatively expansionary even during the austerity years? To answer this question, it is helpful to examine the austerity packages and note that they did not mandate large cuts in government spending. The 1982 austerity package came as part of the franc realignment within the EMS and consisted of three primary components. First, France would seek to hold its budget deficit to 3 percent of the gross national product, a goal that could be attained through tax increases rather than drastic spending cuts (Oatley 1997, 119). Second, France would contract monetarily, slowing money growth from 12 percent in 1982 to 10 percent in 1983. Third, France instituted a series of wages and price controls to reduce inflation.[2] When this package failed to deliver the desired effect, France accepted a second

---

2. Ross's description of French austerity (2001, 26) bears out the story of limited (if any) cuts in government spending by the Socialists.

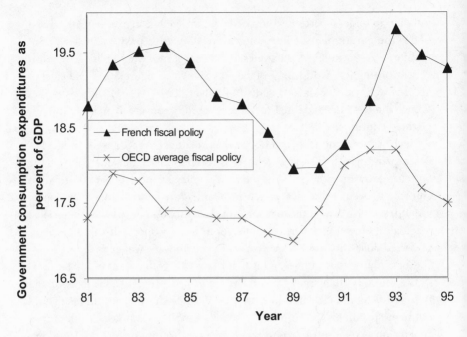

Fig. 19. French Government Spending, 1981–95. (Fiscal policy data from Organization for Economic Cooperation and Development, *Annual National Accounts.*)

austerity program in conjunction with the 1983 franc realignment within the EMS. The second program had four main parts (ibid., 124–25): (1) increased taxes to reduce the budget deficit; (2) limited cuts in government spending, mostly in terms of grants to nationalized sectors; (3) measures to increase the national saving rate; and (4) additional capital controls (e.g., a limit of two thousand francs on foreign exchange transactions for foreign travel).

Often interpreted as a U-turn in Socialist economic policy-making, Goodman (1992, 138) and other scholars have identified Mitterrand's acceptance of austerity as "a true watershed in Socialist economic thought." On this point, the partisan policy mix framework would also identify the austerity programs as watershed events inasmuch as they demonstrate how the Socialists accepted inflation control, along with economic growth, as a top macroeconomic priority given international capital mobility. In this sense, the Socialists finally abandoned any effort to hold an Old Left policy mix with more government spending and lower nominal interest rates.

Others (see, e.g., McNamara 1998, chap. 6) have interpreted these events as consistent with external policy convergence, maintaining that the French left adopted the neoliberal policy prescriptions of the political right. But as figure 20 illustrates, there is a problem with this logic when we identify the combination of less government spending with a lower nominal interest rate as the more neoliberal policy mix. If the French Socialists had wanted to move in this direction, they would have needed tighter fiscal conditions permitting a lower nominal interest rate in order to converge on the low world interest rate. But they did not make this choice: the evidence clearly shows that French government spending under the Socialists remained relatively high on an international basis even during the austerity years. Perhaps it was cut relative to planned levels, and French budget deficits certainly fell as tax revenues grew. But contraction occurred primarily on the monetary side, as French nominal interest rates rose well above the prevailing world rate. This fiscal and monetary combination demonstrates how the French Socialists clearly moved toward a different, more autonomous policy mix.

Exchange Rate Variability

As long as the world interest rate remained low on a nominal basis, the New Left policy mix would be generally incompatible with the external policy goal of exchange rate stability given international capital mobility. Arguably, Mitterrand's new policy mix did offer greater currency stability than would have the Old Left alternative, which had no policy instrument directed toward inflation control. But the New Left policy mix, with its large nominal interest rate differential, could not offer the exchange rate stability promised by the more neoliberal policy mix, with its reduced interest rate differential made possible through cuts in government spending. Indeed, the Socialists continued to face currency pressures within the EMS: a fourth franc realignment occurred in July 1985, a fifth in April 1986, and a sixth in September 1992.[3]

---

3. These realignment events were currency depreciations. As discussed in chapter 3, positive interest rate differentials could be associated with either currency appreciation or currency depreciation, depending on how international investors interpret the interest rate differential. If interpreted as a sign of excess positive returns on capital in the national economy, then positive interest rate differentials would lead to capital inflows and domestic currency appreciation. If interpreted instead as a sign of increasing domestic prices, then a positive interest rate differential would lead to capital outflows and currency depreciation, as it did for the French Socialists. This understanding helps explain why the solution to French exchange rate instability during this period was not simply to raise interest rates even higher, a decision that might have been read as a signal of yet more expected future inflation. Instead, relative exchange rate stability could have been achieved with reduced public spending, since government intervention in the national economy was viewed as one of the major sources of French inflation during this period.

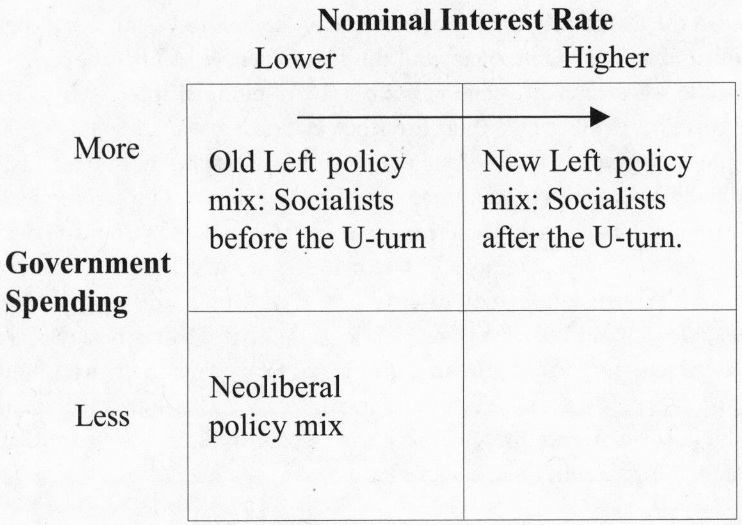

Nominal Interest Rate

	Lower	Higher
More	Old Left policy mix: Socialists before the U-turn	New Left policy mix: Socialists after the U-turn.
Government Spending		
Less	Neoliberal policy mix	

Fig. 20.   The Socialists' New Left Policy Mix

Consequently, Mitterrand's decision to remain inside the exchange rate mechanism of the EMS should not be interpreted as a choice for exchange rate stability over domestic policy autonomy. Howarth (2001, 62) reported in his detailed history of French monetary policy: "One important conclusion can be drawn: that Mitterrand's decision could probably have gone either way on the issue. His rather confused attitudes on desirable economic policy both encouraged and discouraged a float. His European attitudes—support for the *acquis communitaire* and the belief in France's leadership role in Europe—encouraged continued ERM membership, although their importance is difficult to determine. He was convinced less by economic arguments." The decision to remain within the relatively flexible EMS instead reflected Mitterrand's personal goal to maintain French commitments to European institutions. On this point, Howarth further reported, "all of Mitterrand's advisors claim that the most important factor encouraging his decision in favour of the ERM was a long-standing commitment to the European Community, especially given that his knowledge of economics was extremely limited" (78). Jean Peyrelevade, an economic advisor to President Mitterrand, stated, "Allowing the franc to float [i.e., exiting the EMS] would have caused our international partners, who were already suspicious, to doubt the new government's attachment to Europe" (cited in Goodman and Pauly 1993, 71).

Further evidence for the Socialist Party's relative disinterest in exchange rate stability came in 1985, when the French government played only a secondary role in the G-5 Plaza Accord, designed to stabilize the world's major currencies at a time of high exchange rate variability (see Funabashi 1988, 173). The French government later played a major role in constructing the 1987 Louvre Accord, a target-zone system for maintaining currency stability among the G-5 currencies after the Plaza Accord (see Howarth 2001, 100). But it is important to remember that the Louvre Accord was negotiated during a period of cohabitation, when the French political right, who prized exchange rate stability over domestic policy autonomy, governed the national economy.

As President Mitterrand increasingly perceived (perhaps erroneously) the EMS to be a policy straitjacket on the French national economy, he became the vocal leader in searching for a new European monetary regime to replace the EMS. His alternative was the EMU, with a European central bank. Mitterrand reasoned that the EMU's regional central bank with French national representation might be more responsive to the domestic policy preferences represented by the French Socialists than was the German Bundesbank, whose conservative policy decisions arguably dominated the operation of the EMS.

The Socialists and the EMU

Many have interpreted Mitterrand's support for the EMU as proof that the Socialists had finally accepted external policy convergence and exchange rate stability as their dominant economic objectives. But just the opposite appears to be the case. Ross (2001, 29) neatly summarized: "The bottom line was that the French wanted to seize some control of European monetary policy from the German Bundesbank. Others, the Italians in particular, were interested in helping them. The concern was not simply power. What mattered was to construct a new institutional basis for European monetary policy that would be less constrained towards price stability and more growth-friendly." Elgie and Thompson (1998, 127) offered a similar assessment: "Suffice it to say here that Mitterrand promoted monetary union as early as January 1988 because he believed that it would reduce the economic influence of Germany."

Many Socialist Party leaders correctly recognized that the EMU would not offer France greater domestic policy autonomy than did the EMS, and they opposed the new monetary arrangement. Howarth (2002, 185) reported, "there is no evidence of any pro-EMU activity by [Socialist] financial policy advisors close to President Mitterrand or leading Treasury officials prior to June 1988 and the latter continued to oppose the project over the next three years." Indeed, the EMS had permitted the Socialist governments to exercise substantial domestic policy independence, consistent with the assessment that this arrangement represented only "a partial tying of the French government's hands" (Howarth 2001, 191). However, by treating European monetary integration as a French foreign policy issue and, thus, as within the exclusive domain of the French president, Mitterrand simply ignored the opposition within his own party and moved forward on the EMU.

This conclusion is further supported by Ross's evaluation (2001, 45) that the EMU was "*not* a French Socialist project in any partisan terms" but, rather, "the product of a French Socialist President, working in the realm of high diplomatic politics, with the aid of a French Socialist President of the European Commission." Ross continued: "the French Socialists, as a party, did not really confront the realities of EMU in domestic politics until the mid-1990s, at which point EMU was a *fait accompli.* When the confrontation occurred, it was less about the desirability of EMU and more about developing a 'left' domestic-policy package [i.e., maximizing domestic policy autonomy] within the constraints of EMU . . . [suggesting] that EMU will be a negotiable process as it unfolds." In chapter 7, I will return to the subject of how leftist governments have dealt with the policy constraints imposed by the EMU.

2.   The British Conservatives, 1979–96

Conservative Party governance in Britain is an important case to illustrate external policy convergence because it is not an obvious one. Except for a brief period in the early 1990s, Conservative governments have stubbornly stayed outside of European monetary regimes in the post–Bretton Woods era. Thus, for scholars who equate membership in such regimes as a decision for external policy convergence with exchange rate stability and who equate nonmembership as a choice for domestic policy autonomy, the case of the British Conservatives would appear to be an example of the latter choice.

But the Conservatives espoused neoliberal policy ideas and represented the capital-intensive internationally oriented sectors of the British economy. On this point, Philip (1992, 166) concluded, "Clearly industrial and City interests are likely to be most happy with the Conservatives while trade union interests will naturally try to influence Labour's position above all others." Gamble (1994, 246–47) similarly identified the Conservatives as the partisan agent for the internationally oriented sectors of the British economy. He wrote that "by reasserting the traditional international orientation of British economic policy, the [Conservative] government gave priority to the maintenance of the openness of the British economy over the protection of domestic industry." Gamble continued: "This policy favoured those industrial sectors that were already dominated by transnational companies . . . as well as the financial and commercial companies based in the City."

Given this representation, the British Conservatives fit the government partisanship criteria for external policy convergence and stand as a very unlikely case of domestic policy autonomy. Furthermore, Britain's majoritarian electoral system meant that the Conservative governments were not hindered in their choice for policy convergence by political power-sharing arrangements. I will thus here make a three-part case for the British Conservatives as an important example of external policy convergence. The first part will consider the Conservative's neoliberal policy mix. The second part will show how, with their neoliberal policy mix, the Conservatives were able to achieve a relatively stable national currency while remaining outside of the EMS. The third part will briefly examine the period of Labor Party governance beginning in 1997. This examination is important because Labor, rather than the Conservatives, is frequently cast as the British political party that is most interested in external policy convergence. I will show how this interpretation is misleading, making the case for the British Labor Party as a party of domestic policy autonomy.

Toward a Neoliberal Policy Mix

Under the leadership of Margaret Thatcher, the Conservative Party took power in 1979, following five years of Labor Party governance in the United Kingdom. Other than the final years of the Heath government, Thatcher's ascendancy marked the first opportunity for this rightist party to govern its national economy in the post–Bretton Woods era of international capital mobility. Consequently, the Conservatives had to experiment with their policy mix before finding a fiscal and monetary combination that was both feasible given international capital mobility and consistent with their own partisan objectives for exchange rate stability. On the latter issue, it is important to begin with the understanding that the British Conservatives desired exchange rate stability. Thompson (1996, 23) concluded in her study of British monetary policy under the Conservatives, "most fundamentally, Thatcher and Howe [Thatcher's chancellor of the exchequer] were committed to the general aim of exchange rate stability." This important point will be developed in much greater detail shortly.

Facing a situation of high inflation in Britain, the Thatcher government began with a policy mix that was relatively tight on both the fiscal and monetary fronts, effectively directing these two policy instruments toward the same goal of domestic price stability. As I argued in chapter 4, such an Old Right policy mix (with less government spending with a higher national interest rate) quickly becomes unfriendly to international capital, because it tends to stifle economic growth in the national economy. Indeed, with no policy instruments directed at this important economic objective, Britain entered a recession in late 1980. As would be expected, internationally mobile capital exited the British economy, and the pound sterling lost value, especially in 1981 (see Walsh 2000, 497).

This situation forced the Thatcher government to reconsider its Old Right policy mix. Recognizing that one policy instrument (either fiscal or monetary) must be directed toward the objective of economic growth, the Conservatives effectively had two possible options: more government spending with a higher nominal interest rate (the New Left policy mix) or less government spending with a lower interest rate (the neoliberal alternative). As illustrated in figure 21, Thatcher effectively chose the latter, also labeled as the New Right policy mix. Indeed, Seldon and Collins (2000, 66) concluded, "Thatcher herself came to accept the recession of 1980/81 had been aggravated by a too tight monetary policy." But the need for continued inflation control meant that British fiscal policy should remain relatively tight. As an explicit means to coordinate their fiscal and monetary policy choices (consistent with the logic of deliberate policy counterbalancing), the Conservatives introduced the new Medium Term Financial Strategy.

The new Conservative government faced some initial difficulty in implementing their plans for fiscal contraction. British government spending relative to GDP did not fall as quickly as the Conservatives had planned (see Boix 1998, 163). But much of this difficulty was certainly due to the recessionary environment in Britain. Hall (1986, 116) noted, "the high public spending to GDP ratios [in the early Thatcher years] reflect a sluggish denominator as well as a rising numerator." The numerator also rose in the early 1980s, because the Thatcher government "increased expenditure on such traditional Conservative priorities as defense, law and order, and agriculture" (ibid.).

As the British economy improved, however, the Conservatives' contractionary fiscal stance became more apparent. Nigel Lawson, who replaced Howe as the chancellor of the exchequer in 1983, began budgeting based on a "slower rate of growth for public spending than the sustainable growth rate of the economy as a whole, with the result that public expenditure would steadily decline as a share of GDP" (Lawson 1992, 305–6). Over the long run, the Conservatives were certainly successful in cutting government expenditures relative to GDP.

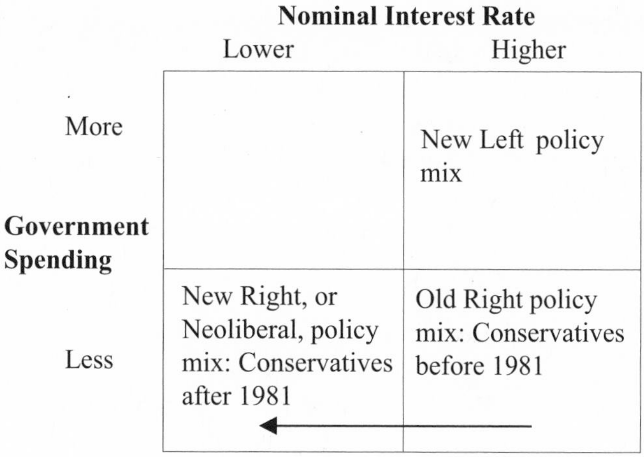

Nominal Interest Rate

	Lower	Higher
More		New Left policy mix
Government Spending		
Less	New Right, or Neoliberal, policy mix: Conservatives after 1981	Old Right policy mix: Conservatives before 1981

Fig. 21.   The Conservatives' Neoliberal Policy Mix

Seldon and Collins (2000, 67) reported: "[total p]ublic spending fell from 44% of GDP in 1979 to just under 40% by 1990, a considerable achievement when it is remembered that expenditure rose significantly in many other European countries over this period."

While describing the Conservatives' fiscal policy stance as generally contractionary is not particularly controversial, many readers may be surprised at the relative looseness of British monetary policy beginning in 1981. Several detailed studies of British monetary policy during this period document how the Conservative government consistently overshot their stated monetary policy targets (see, e.g., Cobham 2002, chaps. 3–4; Temperton 1991), indicating a looser monetary policy measured in terms of money supply. Hall (1986, 118), for example, showed that sterling M3 growth, the Conservatives' preferred monetary supply indicator, consistently went above or to the high end of the target range from 1979 to 1985. Similarly, Talani (2000, 104) presented data from the Bank of England documenting the steady growth of sterling M3 stock during the entire first decade of Conservative Party governance.

In 1985, the Conservatives effectively ended money supply targeting (see Cobham 2002, 53). But even of the period when they did state money supply targets in the early 1980s, Minford (1993, 430) argued that "the implementation of [British] monetary policy has been through interest-rate changes rather than through monetary base control."[4] With regard to national interest rates, low rates were a very important part of Thatcher's privatization program to encourage private investment in formerly state-owned enterprises. Lawson (chancellor of the exchequer for 1983–89) later stated: "low interest rates had an unfailing appeal for Margaret [Thatcher]. Despite her reputation as a diehard opponent of inflation, and her dislike of it was undoubtedly genuine, she was almost always in practice anxious to reduce interest rates" (cited in Thompson 1996, 60).

Exchange Rate Stability outside the ERM

As long as the Conservatives held their neoliberal policy mix, membership in the exchange rate mechanism of the EMS would be a very feasible policy option for the United Kingdom. Thompson (1996, 48) argued: "the Prime Minister and Chancellor had accepted . . . that monetary and fiscal policy could be used for different purposes. In assigning the former to the exchange rate [i.e., a low nominal interest rate to minimize the national interest rate differential] and the latter to controlling domestic expansion [i.e., inflation control], they formulated policy in the way most compatible with ERM membership." Yet they remained outside the institution.

Many officials within the Thatcher government favored joining the ERM, including those at the Treasury (particularly Lawson) and the Bank of England. Thatcher's own views regarding European exchange rate regime membership have often been misunderstood. Thatcher had announced herself as an early supporter of the EMS concept. As the member states of the European Community (EC) drew up plans for the new fixed exchange rate regime in 1978, the then-governing Labor Party announced that Britain would not join the multilateral currency arrangement. The Conservatives in opposition criticized the unwillingness of the prime minister, James Callaghan, to join the EMS, with Thatcher lamenting, "This is a sad day for Europe." She complained that Labor was content to have "Britain classified among the poorer and least influential countries in the EC" (cited in Thompson 1996, 14; see also Gamble and Kelly 2002, 102).

Once in power, however, Thatcher changed her tune, voicing opposition to membership in the exchange rate mechanism of the EMS. But her opposition

---

4. This illustrates the important point (made in chap. 4) that the money supply is endogenous to the short-term interest rate. Thus, the best indicator of a state's chosen monetary policy orientation is a policy interest rate, rather than a measure of the money supply.

was due not to any lack of interest in exchange rate stability per se (indeed, just the opposite was true) but, rather, to concerns about participation in an exchange rate regime viewed as antidollar[5] and about the perceived loss of British national sovereignty to this and other such European institutions. As Oatley argued, though "Thatcher was in the minority [among Conservatives] opposing membership," she nonetheless "managed to force an outcome" that kept Britain out of the ERM until 1990 (Oatley 1997, 73). Thus, the Conservatives were "operating an economic policy similar in substance to ERM membership [less government spending for a lower nominal interest rate and interest rate differential] but at Thatcher's insistence outside the system and in tandem with a relatively isolationist EC policy" (Thompson 1996, 31).

Some scholars (see Talani 2000, 73) have expressed surprise at the "complete silence of the societal and economic actors" favoring British monetary convergence and exchange rate stability on the subject of ERM membership during the early 1980s. As Thompson documented, "[t]he City [financial services] wanted the security of reduced exchange rate volatility and a counterinflationary discipline," as did the "[m]ultinational companies operating in Britain [international exporters]," but that "it could not be said that either sector saw [ERM] membership as imperative to their interests" (Thompson 1996, 56). Yet it is not hard to understand why this would be the case, since the Conservative governments, for the most part, held a policy mix consistent with the goal of exchange rate stability. Thus, lobbying their rightist partisan agents for this desired economic objective was simply unnecessary given that the Conservatives were already actively working for and, indeed, achieving external currency stability during this period.[6]

However, British interest rates and interest rate differentials did increase in 1984 and 1985, leading to greater exchange rate variability for the pound sterling (see fig. 22). Predictably, when the Conservatives did not effectively work for external monetary convergence and exchange rate stability, these internationally oriented societal principals began to lobby their partisan agents on behalf of ERM membership as a possible solution to increased external currency volatility. Thompson (1996, 40) documented the lobbying pressure as the sterling's variability grew in 1984–85: "in the City, firms and individuals were becoming increasingly interested in ERM entry. In August 1984, the Lloyd's Bank of Economic Bulletin argued that the fall in sterling in the previ-

5. During the 1980s, the United States was Britain's largest export market, just ahead of the German market.

6. On this point, see Bearce 2003, 397–98.

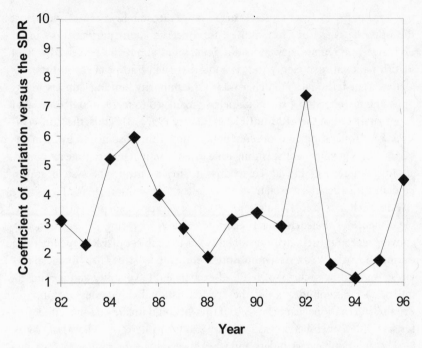

Fig. 22.   British Exchange Rate Variability, 1982–96. (Exchange rate data
from International Monetary Fund, *International Financial Statistics*.)

ous month could have been avoided inside the ERM. Three months later a
group of City bankers and economists published a report highlighting the
benefits of membership." Thompson continued: "During 1985 a succession of
business groups, economic organizations and financial commentators came
out in favor of ERM entry. . . . The sterling crisis had brought the issue of currency volatility to a head. Previously, firms valued exchange rate stability, but
were confident that it could be better achieved outside rather than inside the
ERM" (51).

To diffuse this lobbying pressure, the Conservatives began to shadow the
German currency beginning in 1986, unofficially pegging the value of the
pound sterling to the deutsche mark without announcing publicly any specific
targets. This shadowing was understood as a "quasi form of membership" that
"committed the government to exchange rate stability against the ERM anchor
currency" and "used both monetary policy and reserve intervention to achieve
that end" (Thompson 1996, 92). Within the British government, Lawson

tended to view shadowing as a dry run for eventual ERM entry, while Thatcher viewed it as an alternative to entry. The 1987 Louvre Accord further reinforced Britain's shadowing policy, as the Thatcher government agreed to a de facto G-5 target zone, which included the deutsche mark. As Boix (1998, 197) correctly noted, this shadowing policy would not have been effective without "substantial cuts in interest rates," which were made possible by reduced public spending under Conservative Party governance.

Despite helping to stabilize the British currency from 1986 to 1988 (as shown in fig. 22), the shadowing policy engendered strong criticism from EMS governments that Britain was free riding on European monetary institutions. Such criticism manifested itself as external political pressure on the Conservative government to join the ERM formally. When the sterling's variability increased again in 1989 and 1990, the Conservative government also came under internal pressure from their internationally oriented societal principals with preferences for exchange rate stability.

This combination of external and internal political pressure effectively forced the Conservatives to work even harder on behalf of exchange rate stability. In 1990, Thatcher's government offered the hard ecu as an alternative to the French-led plan for the EMU. The Conservatives' hard European Currency Unit (ecu) strategy had proposed to fix the value of an ecu to each of the EC national currencies and to create a European monetary fund to issue hard ecus, which would then circulate parallel to the national currencies. But coming from the Thatcher government, which had elected to remain outside of (and even to free ride on) existing European monetary institutions, the hard ecu proposal received a very cold reception from other EC member states.

Thatcher then relented on her opposition to ERM membership. Talani (2000, 133) attributes this change to political pressure from the "factions of British capital, the productive [exporters] and the financial one [international investors]." Similarly, despite all the Conservative rhetoric about ERM membership as an anti-inflationary lock, Cobham's (2002, 74) survey of British monetary policy noted that Britain's entry into the institution was more likely due to the Conservative's interest in and societal pressure for an "increase in exchange rate stability." Thus, in October 1990, Britain finally joined the exchange rate mechanism of the EMS.

Unfortunately for the Conservatives and their societal principals, Thatcher chose to join the institution at a time when the British pound sterling was overvalued. The following month, in November 1990, John Major replaced Thatcher as the Conservative Party prime minister. Major and his chancellor of the exchequer, Norman Lamont, rigidly maintained Thatcher's tight fiscal policy, perhaps tightening more for inflation control than ERM membership actually required. Even facing a recession, Major and Lamont proposed budgetary cuts, leaving a looser monetary policy as the only possible economic growth option. However, as Germany raised interest rates in the wake of reunification and as the interest rate differential between the two countries expanded, the sterling faced considerable depreciation pressures. The Bank of England's active intervention into international currency markets delayed a crisis temporarily until September 1992, when circumstances forced Britain (and Italy) to exit the ERM.

Given the Conservatives' interest in exchange rate stability, their exit from the ERM represented a humiliating political defeat. Indeed, Gamble and Kelly (2002, 103) identify this episode as an effective death blow to the pro-European wing of the Conservative Party. The same authors also speculate that had the Conservatives not experienced such an embarrassing failure within the ERM, the Conservative leadership would likely have recommended British entry into the EMU. To this day, there remain EMU enthusiasts within the Conservative Party (see Pilkington 2001, 187–93). These include Kenneth Clarke, who narrowly lost a party leadership struggle to Iain Duncan Smith in 2001.

Indeed, in the early 1990s, the new Conservative prime minister John Major expressed his enthusiasm for the EMU convergence criteria (see Elgie and Thompson 1998, 75). Other than Britain's ERM nonmembership, the Conservatives managed to satisfy the neoliberal EMU convergence criteria without serious difficulty (see Pilkington 2001, 189). In fact, despite ERM nonmembership, Major's Conservative government achieved a remarkable record of exchange rate stability after 1992. Figure 22 reveals a very stable British currency especially from 1993 to 1995, before the Conservatives finally lost power in early 1997.

Given these facts, it is important to address whether or not Conservative governance in Britain fits the "fear of floating" phenomenon (see Calvo and Reinhart 2002). As discussed in chapter 2, this argument from economics describes why de jure floaters, such as Britain, might behave as de facto fixers: external factors make the costs of domestic policy autonomy simply unbearable. But the case analysis here shows why the Conservatives' move toward external policy convergence and exchange rate stability represented a deliberate policy choice. To the extent that the Conservatives were constrained in this policy choice, the operative constraints were less external and more internal, coming from internationally oriented groups within British society.

This understanding explains why British external policy convergence is not consistent with the larger argument of systematic monetary policy convergence. The Conservatives chose to move in this direction even as other OECD governments made different policy choices with international capital mobility. Thus, the British Conservatives fit nicely with the theme of monetary policy divergence in the post–Bretton Woods era.

Putting Labor Party Governance in Context

At this point, it becomes useful to shift gears and briefly consider the British Labor Party, which took power in 1997 under the leadership of Tony Blair. I have just argued that the British Conservatives—if not in words, then certainly in deeds—were a party choosing external policy convergence and exchange rate stability. What is the policy choice of the British Labor Party, and what are the preferences of its key societal supporters?

With regard to the latter, the British Labor Party continues to receive much of its political support from the traditional working classes. While some have argued that there has been a class-partisan dealignment in Britain, Denver (1998, 200, 211) provided strong evidence to the contrary, concerning voting patterns in both the 1992 and 1997 elections. Similarly, Fielding (1999, 120) presented data on Labor Party membership, concluding that "the new members were socially not very different from those who joined before Blair." If anything, Fielding added, the Labor Party's "new recruits were slightly more likely to be working class and male." With the decline of heavy industry and the import-competing manufacturing sector, the British Labor Party has also looked for political support from the growing service sector, which remains largely nontradable due to Britain's island economy. This means that even as the new Labor government finds its political base to be in services and not in import-competing manufacturing, the leftist Labor Party would still be expected to work for domestic policy autonomy.

But given Blair's apparent enthusiasm for the EMU, at least relative to other British political leaders, conventional wisdom has tended to treat the Labor Party as the British political party most interested in external policy convergence. I argue that this conventional wisdom is somewhat misguided, as Blair's support for the EMU stems not from any Labor Party preference for exchange rate stability over domestic policy autonomy but, rather, from Blair's intense personal desire to increase British influence on the European continent. One observer recently wrote: "Mr Blair, in contrast, has always seen the politics of the euro as a question of influence rather than sovereignty. His ambition is to 'lead' in Europe, and his supporters have always argued that such an ambition can never be fully realized if Britain continues to stand aside from the euro."[7]

7. See *Economist* 2003b.

Other observers have taken an even more skeptical view of the Labor Party's apparent support for the EMU on the Continent, treating Blair's vocal support for the EMU as merely a "political device to counter the [increasingly anti-EMU] direction taken by the Conservatives" (Pilkington 2001, 183). Indeed, British entry into the EMU is opposed by much of the rest of the Labor Party government, including officials at the Treasury and the Foreign Office and many Labor members of Parliament.[8] Despite such opposition, Blair has thus far successfully managed to downplay the EMU and other European policy divisions among Labor Party leaders. Pilkington (ibid., 192) wrote, "New Labour as led by Tony Blair, and with a whole host of spin doctors to manipulate opinion, has been a lot better at masking dissent within the party than the Conservatives and European issues do not figure very prominently in Labour's strategy."

Consistent with this latter point is the fact that the new Labor Party government, not the outgoing Conservatives, officially rejected British participation in the EMU (see Gamble and Kelly 2002, 104). While the Conservatives negotiated the opt-out for Britain at Maastricht in 1992, the Labor government effectively exercised the EMU opt-out in 1997. Furthermore, the new Labor government set up a series of the tests that the British economy would need to meet before any referendum on EMU membership could even be presented to British voters. In June 2003, after several years of speculation, Gordon Brown, the Labor Party's chancellor of the exchequer, finally announced that the British economy had failed four of the five tests. Thus, an EMU referendum (and British entry into the project) appears very unlikely to occur under Labor Party governance.

The reluctance of Gordon Brown and other Labor Party leaders to enter the EMU appears to stem, in large part, from the expected loss of fiscal policy autonomy following from the Stability and Growth Pact, which makes EMU governments running a budget deficit in excess of 3 percent of GDP potentially subject to fines of up to 0.5 percent of GDP. Deficits remain fairly low in Britain after years of spending cuts under Conservative governance, but Labor supporters in the domestically oriented sectors of the British economy have strong expectations for more public goods and services to be supplied by the state.[9] Thus, it is not surprising that the Labor Party has increased government spending by about 4 percent a year, with a particular focus on health, education, and transportation.[10]

---

8. See *Economist* 2003a.
9. On this point, see *Economist* 2002b.
10. See *Economist* 2001c.

The Labor Party's fiscal policy autonomy has been quietly accompanied by an increasingly autonomous monetary policy stance. Just after taking power in 1997, Blair granted greater independence to the Bank of England, which has helped to keep nominal interest rates low in the domestic economy and to minimize the extent of monetary counterbalancing necessary for fiscal expansion, consistent with the results presented in chapter 5. But under Labor Party governance, British monetary policy has been used almost exclusively for domestic price stability. Indeed, in his survey of British monetary policy through 2000, Cobham's statistical analysis (2002, 117) showed that British interest rates under the Blair government have varied only in response to domestic factors—mostly that of inflation. This finding contrasts sharply with monetary policy under Conservative governance, when the movement of British interest rates also reflected international factors as Thatcher and Major sought to reduce their interest rate differential with the United States and Germany (see ibid., 67, 105). In short, the international character of British monetary policy has effectively disappeared with the more autonomous policy choices made by Labor Party governments.

The two case studies discussed in this chapter illustrate a number of important theoretical arguments. First, they demonstrate how OECD governments have coordinated spending decisions with interest rate policy. In the case of the French Socialists, one can observe deliberate monetary counterbalancing in an effort to offset the inflationary pressures associated with greater government spending. For the British Conservatives, counterbalancing went in the opposite direction: less government spending facilitated a lower nominal interest rate and reduced the interest rate differential.

Second, these cases show how a government's policy mix affects national exchange rate stability. The New Left policy mix, with larger nominal interest rate differentials, made exchange rate stability difficult for the French Socialists to achieve, even with all the supposed advantages made possible by continued membership in the exchange rate mechanism of the EMS. Conversely, the neoliberal policy mix generally held by the British Conservatives facilitated exchange rate stability, even though Britain remained outside of this institution. These prominent examples help illustrate how a government's policy mix choice offers a better explanation for national exchange rate stability than does its (non)membership in regional monetary or exchange rate regimes.

Finally, these two cases illustrate partisan divergence in terms of fiscal and monetary policy instruments and, as a result, the policy outcome of exchange rate stability. International capital mobility in the post–Bretton Woods era may have reinforced partisan convergence in terms of other economic outcomes, such as growth and actual inflation. But partisan governments representing different societal interest groups can meet these macroeconomic outcomes using a different combination of fiscal and monetary policies, provided that they are properly coordinated. Such policy mix divergence engenders further partisan differences in terms of domestic monetary policy autonomy and exchange rate variability.

CHAPTER 7

Expanding the Argument

This final chapter has two purposes. The first is simply to summarize the major arguments and findings in the previous chapters. But most of the final pages are devoted to a second purpose: discussing some broader implications of the theory and results presented in this book. In particular, I will relate the book's basic argument about policy divergence to a major academic debate in the field of international relations and also to an important policy question in Western Europe. On the academic side, the theory and evidence presented in this book speak directly to certain conclusions that have emerged from two decades of debate concerning international cooperation theory. On the policy side, these findings make some interesting and somewhat pessimistic predictions concerning the future of the Economic and Monetary Union on the European continent. Finally, this chapter concludes by discussing how the analysis presented in this book could be extended beyond the OECD countries.

I. Summary of the Basic Argument

This book has been organized around two primary research questions. First, given sound operational measures for domestic monetary policy autonomy, can we find much evidence of systematic monetary policy convergence among the OECD states in the post–Bretton Woods era? Second, given no evidence of such systematic policy convergence, can we explain the related patterns of policy divergence, including monetary policy divergence, since the early 1970s?

In many ways, the monetary convergence hypothesis represents the last stand for the broader theory of macroeconomic policy convergence, which was first advanced by political scientists in the early 1990s. While the broad macroeconomic policy convergence logic has been widely attacked—and even disproved—in a number of issue areas (notably with regard to government spending and other fiscal policy decisions), the narrower hypothesis of monetary policy convergence has remained a conventional wisdom within certain circles of political science. Indeed, even scholars who have been critical of the broad policy convergence proposition have acknowledged that monetary convergence represents the strongest case, or issue area, for the broader theory of macroeconomic policy convergence with international capital mobility.[1]

With regard to this book's first research question, chapter 2 discussed a number of theoretical problems facing confirmation of the systematic monetary policy convergence hypothesis. Chapter 3 showed how little empirical support this hypothesis eventually receives once we employ sound operational measures for domestic monetary policy autonomy and the related concept of national exchange rate stability. As one scholar wrote, it is desirable to be in the position to "either write the first article on a subject or the last one" (Schrodt 2004, 886). Clearly, this study has not been the first critique of the monetary convergence hypothesis, but it does have the potential to be the last. When this misleading monetary policy convergence proposition can be put to rest (once and for all), the discipline can move ahead with explaining related patterns of policy divergence.

After chapter 2 showed how the post–Bretton Woods era is better characterized by the concept of monetary policy divergence, the next three chapters explored national differences with regard to nominal interest rates and exchange rate stability, addressing this book's second research question. Chapter 4 linked the evidence of monetary policy divergence to the well-established fact of fiscal policy divergence among the advanced industrial democracies since the early 1970s, offering the policy mix framework. When governments spend more for economic growth with public goods and/or income redistribution, they must also raise nominal interest rates for inflation control. A higher domestic interest rate tends to increase the national interest rate differential, leading to greater exchange rate variability. This policy mix framework shows how exchange rate stability can be treated as endogenous to the government's spending and interest rate decisions, thus helping to explain the observed disconnect between de jure and de facto exchange rate regimes.

Chapter 5 then explored certain determinants of government spending, nominal interest rates, national interest rate differentials, and exchange rate variability in the post–Bretton Woods era. The statistical results showed the importance of government partisanship, a finding that runs contrary to most policy convergence arguments, which predicted that partisan factors are largely

---

1. On this point, see Garrett 1998a, 802; Drezner 2001, 75.

irrelevant in terms of policy outcomes and even policy instruments. For certain indicators, such as economic growth and actual inflation, partisan differences may well be insignificant, but this fact does not mean that partisan governments have also converged in their use of fiscal and monetary policy instruments and the related policy outcome of exchange rate stability. Chapter 6 further illustrated the concept of partisan policy divergence with regard to government spending, nominal interest rates, and exchange rate variability by focusing on two important case examples: the French Socialists and the British Conservatives.

2. International Cooperation Theory and Macroeconomic Policy Coordination

The partisan argument advanced in chapters 5 and 6 concerning exchange rate stability and the related use of fiscal and monetary policy instruments has some important implications for established international cooperation theory. To understand why this is the case, it is useful to start at the very beginning of the international cooperation debate. Scholars working on this broad topic have always been careful with their definition of *cooperation,* with the term usually defined by Keohane's classic description (1984, 51): "when actors adjust their behavior to the actual or anticipated preferences of others, through a process of policy coordination."

Cooperation is thus obviously not *discord,* which occurs when actors do not adjust their behavior. But it is also different from *harmony.* Axelrod and Keohane (1986, 226) later stated on the subject: "Cooperation is not equivalent to harmony. Harmony requires complete identity of interests, but cooperation can only take place in situations that contain a mixture of conflicting and complementary interests." In *Cooperation under Anarchy,* Oye (1986, 7) made a very similar point, cautioning that scholars must first rule out a simple harmony of national interests to demonstrate convincingly that genuine international cooperation has occurred.

Scholars have regularly identified the 1978 Bonn summit and the 1985 Plaza Accord as examples of genuine international cooperation.[2] Indeed, as Sterling-Folker (2002, chap. 4) argued, much of international cooperation theory, especially the neoliberal institutionalist version, has been built on these examples of great powers involved in macroeconomic policy coordination. Yet the partisan

---

2. See, for example, Gilpin 1987, chap. 4; Putnam and Bayne 1987; Putnam 1988; Putnam and Henning 1989; Webb 1991; Cooper 1994; Webb 1995.

argument offered here suggests that these events may not be as cooperative as many have argued. This is true for two reasons. First, much of the macroeconomic policy coordination can be explained by a simple harmony of partisan economic interests. Second, where partisan economic interests were not aligned, discord emerged, with notable defections from international cooperation. To illustrate these points, I will first discuss the 1978 Bonn Summit and then the 1985 Plaza Accord.

The 1978 Bonn Summit

The 1978 Bonn summit is an example of fiscal policy coordination among the G-3 (Group of Three) governments. At this time, two of the G-3 economies were governed by the political left: the Democratic Carter administration in the United States and the Social Democratic Schmidt government in West Germany. A rightist government (the LDP) held power in Japan, the other G-3 economy. The partisan model presented here makes two predictions with regard to such macroeconomic policy coordination. First, there should be a relative harmony of interest between the United States and West Germany, especially with regard to fiscal expansion. Second, Japan should resist any outside pressure from these leftist governments for increases in government spending and should ultimately defect on the terms of the summit agreement.

There is support for both of these predictions. With regard to the first, Putnam (1988, 428) acknowledged in his case study of cooperation at the 1978 Bonn summit: "the Bonn deal was not forced on a reluctant . . . Germany. In fact, officials in the Chancellor's Office and the Economics Ministry, as well as in the Social Democratic party and trade unions, had argued privately in early 1978 that further [fiscal] stimulus was domestically desirable, particularly in view of the approaching 1980 elections." Other scholars, such as Iida (1993), have suggested that the Schmidt government was reluctant to cooperate with Carter's demand for fiscal expansion. The German government had to be persuaded; hence, the Bonn summit represented real international cooperation, not just a harmony of interests. But Putnam (1988, 429) also wrote: "Publicly, Helmut Schmidt posed as reluctant to the end. Only his closest advisors suspected the truth: that the chancellor 'let himself be pushed' into a policy that he privately favored." Furthermore, Iida (1993, 447) conceded: "Hans Matthoffer, who replaced Hans Apel as [Schmidt's] finance minister at the beginning of 1978, was much more audacious in fiscal policy making. Presumably, his view of fiscal policy was much closer to that of Keynesians in the Carter administration."

With regard to the second prediction, there is ample evidence of an LDP defection after the Bonn agreement. Despite the promise by the Japanese prime minister Takeo Fukuda to achieve a domestic growth target of 7 percent, Henning (1994, 128) concluded that Japanese expansion, if it occurred at all, took place only on the monetary side, consistent with the LDP's partisan preference for monetary expansion over fiscal expansion. Cargill, Hutchison, and Ito (1997, 187) argued: "The Ministry of Finance is indeed conservative in the sense of being very reluctant to use fiscal policy to manage aggregate demand [i.e., promote economic growth]. This reluctance to use discretionary policy, known in Japan as the 'Ministry of Finance view,' may be characterized as anti-Keynesian. It is rooted in the early postwar experience with near-hyperinflation and in the wild inflation [of the early 1970s]." As a Japanese government official stated, the LDP finance ministry "never compromises to foreigners on fiscal policy, only on monetary policy" (quoted from Henning 1994, 174). Thus, Smyser (1993, 18) concluded: "Fukuda did not stimulate the Japanese economy as much as he had promised. Germany stood alone in carrying her share of the bargain." This latter fact can be explained by a simple harmony of partisan interest between the then-leftist governments in the United States and West Germany.

Discord between the rightist government in Japan and its leftist counterpart in the United States went even further at the 1978 Bonn summit. In the year before the summit, the Japanese government had been pushing the United States to make greater efforts toward exchange rate stability: "Fukuda argued that without a stable exchange rate system, domestic expansion was undesirable and achieving world economic stability improbable" (Suzuki 2000, 82). But with regard to this external policy objective, the Carter administration was largely indifferent, as the partisan policy mix framework predicts for such leftist governments. U.S. Treasury secretary Michael Blumenthal publicly stated on the subject: "I would like to see a free floating—apart from smoothing out ragged movements—and allow the exchange rate between the dollar and the yen and the dollar and the Deutschmark to settle down where it does in that context. Whether or not that point has been reached, time will tell, and I would be quite happy to live with whatever the result is."[3] Indeed, Sterling-Folker (2002, 154) concluded, "U.S. policymakers [would] make no commitment to stabilizing the dollar because they were suspicious of Japan's real commitment to the growth target." Given the Carter administration's relative disinterest in exchange rate stability as a policy end in itself, "[e]xchange rates were largely

3. Quoted in Rowen 1977.

neglected as a topic of conversation at the [Bonn] summit" (Henning 1994, 268).

The 1985 Plaza Accord

Exchange rates were the main topic of conversation at the Plaza Hotel in New York seven years later. The Plaza Accord that was reached in September 1985 emerged out of U.S.-Japanese negotiations. Both the United States and Japan were governed at this time by rightist parties with strong ideological interests in exchange rate stability and with powerful interest group pressures to work harder on behalf of this external policy objective. Their negotiations proceeded relatively smoothly, largely due to this partisan compatibility. Suzuki (2000, 141) wrote on this point, "part of the explanation undoubtedly rested in the fact that Japan was now negotiating with a predominantly conservative group of foreign leaders"—beginning with the United States and later including West Germany and the United Kingdom.

There was certainly more friction in the negotiations leading to the Plaza Accord when the United States and Japan finally approached their European partners. Funabashi (1988, chap. 5), for example, has written about the pre-Plaza disagreements between the United States and West Germany. But as his account makes clear, there was no disagreement about the goal of achieving greater exchange rate stability for the world's major currencies. Indeed, the Germans had long been asking the Reagan administration to pay greater attention to the dollar's movements and steady appreciation. Instead, U.S.-German disagreements centered on the details of planned multilateral intervention into international currency markets. Since West Germany had already conducted unilateral interventions directed at realigning the dollar-mark exchange rate, the Kohl government simply wanted to see the second Reagan administration assume a greater share of the joint intervention effort.

As the partisan model presented here predicts, these rightist governments would eventually succeed in reaching and then executing an agreement for exchange rate stability. But such an agreement would not necessarily indicate genuine international cooperation; instead, it reflects, to a very large extent, a partisan harmony of interests. Perhaps the Plaza Accord would represent cooperation if a leftist government with different policy interests had put its domestic concerns aside and worked with the rightist governments in the United States, Japan, West Germany, and the United Kingdom for external currency stability. But, on this point, it is again worth noting that France—the only G-5 economy led by a leftist government at this time—played only a "secondary" role in the 1985 Plaza Accord (see Funabashi 1988, 173).

To be certain, the French government became more active in working for exchange rate stability and was instrumental in achieving the 1987 Louvre Accord. But this fact does not indicate Socialist cooperation with the rightist G-5 partners. As mentioned briefly in chapter 6, it instead reflects the logic of French cohabitation, a period from March 1986 to March 1988 during which the French political right governed the national economy, with Jacques Chirac as prime minister. Similarly, U.S.-Japanese monetary coordination during this period can be attributed to a harmony of interests. Henning (1994, 156) wrote: "The perception is now commonplace [especially] in Japan that interest rates were kept at all-time lows throughout 1988 out of deference to the Reagan administration and international cooperation. . . . But there is no evidence of either overt or covert American pressure on Japan [at this time]."

3. The Uncertain Future of the EMU

The analysis presented in this book should be of interest not only to academic theorists, as discussed earlier, but also to national and regional policymakers in Europe and elsewhere. The policy mix framework speaks directly about the potential viability of the Economic and Monetary Union (EMU) in Europe. Unfortunately for euro-optimists, its logic suggests that the EMU faces an uncertain and potentially problematic future. This is true not because the EMU is a weak and flexible institution (as were the European Snake and the EMS) but because the EMU entails a wide array of domestic policy constraints, some of which have clearly been difficult for many European leftist governments to accept, while others are becoming increasingly unpalatable even for certain European rightist governments. It is also important to discuss further this new regional monetary institution because my analysis of European monetary cooperation necessarily focused on the region's first two post–Bretton Woods monetary regimes, the primary institutions studied by scholars first advancing the monetary convergence hypothesis in the early 1990s. The European Snake and the EMS were shown in earlier chapters to have functioned as relatively flexible monetary arrangements, allowing member states to retain a significant measure of domestic policy autonomy within these regimes.[4]

The EMU, however, appears to be a very different animal. Participation in this third post–Bretton Woods European monetary regime required governments to give up their national currencies, adopt a common regional currency, and take the interest rate set by the European Central Bank. EMU membership

---

4. Indeed, the flexibility of the EMS is often cited as a primary reason for its longevity (see, e.g., Froot and Rogoff 1991, 307).

(unlike that of the European Snake or the EMS) would seem to represent a clear policy choice for regional exchange rate stability, with the corresponding loss of domestic monetary autonomy. Indeed, EMU domestic policy constraints potentially extend beyond the monetary side. To preserve the contractionary fiscal policies facilitated by the Maastricht convergence criteria, the 1997 Stability and Growth Pact required, at least in principal, that EMU governments keep their national budget deficit below 3 percent of GDP or face huge fines of up to 0.5 percent of GDP as a penalty for excess fiscal looseness.

As the Maastricht convergence criteria and the Stability and Growth Pact illustrate, the EMU came about on largely neoliberal policy terms. This is not surprising, since the final plans for the project were drawn up in the early 1990s, when the political right dominated national governments in Western Europe. This is a very important historical fact, since it helps explain how an institution pushing for neoliberal policy convergence could emerge in the post–Bretton Woods era, which has been characterized by macroeconomic policy divergence.[5]

This understanding—that the EMU was constructed to facilitate the political right's preferred macroeconomic policy objectives—suggests that right-wing and right-centrist governments would enthusiastically decide to join the EMU, while left-wing governments would decide to remain outside the new European monetary institution. Indeed, this is almost precisely what happened in 1997, the so-called drop dead date for entry into the third and final stage of the EMU (see fig. 23).[6] Nineteen ninety-seven was the year that the convergence criteria had to be satisfied; thus, if any government was to be initially excluded, as was Greece, it would be based on its continuing economic policy divergence at that point in time.[7] Likewise, if any government was to play its opt-out card, as did Britain, this option would have to be activated in 1997.

Of course, leftist governments returned to power in certain countries where right-wing governments had already made commitments to enter into the EMU. Two important cases are Germany, with its Social Democratic and Green Party coalition government that assumed power in 1998, and France, with its Socialist cohabitation government beginning in late 1997. Why did these new leftist governments not renege on the EMU commitments made by

5. I thank an anonymous reviewer for pushing me to acknowledge more explicitly this apparent contradiction.

6. The exception is Portugal, which was led by a leftist government in 1997 but nonetheless decided to enter into the EMU. However, Portugal was one of the first EMU member states to run afoul of the Stability and Growth Pact, a problem that will be discussed shortly.

7. Greece was permitted to join the EMU in 2001, but it now appears that Greece had misled the European Union about the extent of its fiscal policy divergence.

	Enter EMU	Outside EMU
Right-centrist government in power in 1997	Germany, France, Italy, the Netherlands, Belgium, Luxembourg, Ireland, Spain, Austria, Finland	
Leftist government in power in 1997	Portugal	Britain, Denmark, Greece, Sweden

Fig. 23.   1997 Decisions concerning the EMU

the previous right-wing governments? In the French case, this would have been a very difficult political decision to execute, since cohabitation meant that French foreign policy—with the EMU being treated as a foreign policy issue (as discussed in chap. 6)—was controlled by the rightist French president Jacques Chirac, although there is evidence that the Socialist prime minister Lionel Jospin nonetheless considered ways to keep the French national economy outside of the EMU (see Ross 2001, 38–45).

For other leftist governments, such as the Schroeder government in Germany, there was arguably no immediate need to renege on the country's EMU commitment. In the late 1990s, and perhaps uniquely so, economic growth in Europe (and elsewhere in the global North) was relatively strong, and inflationary pressures were surprisingly weak. Under such favorable economic conditions (i.e., noninflationary growth), there were correspondingly weak societal demands for domestic policy autonomy, and the choice for neoliberal policy convergence appeared relatively costless, at least in the short run. Thus, it was possible for certain leftist governments to stomach the prospect of neoliberal EMU policy constraints in order to demonstrate their commitment to European institutions, norms, and the broader regional integration process. Of course, for other leftist governments, arguably less committed to these European goals, the potential EMU policy constraints were unacceptable even with noninflationary growth, leading Britain, Sweden, and Denmark to stay outside the Eurozone.

The favorable economic environment that existed in the late 1990s has changed markedly in the new century, as economic growth in Europe declined, unemployment rose, and inflationary pressures returned.[8] Not surprisingly,

8. See, for example, *Economist* 2004b.

societal demands for domestic policy autonomy have remounted. Several European governments—including, but not limited to, those on the political left—have hit the fiscal limits set by the Stability and Growth Pact.[9] Frustrated with this situation, European Commission president Romano Prodi publicly predicted a future "crisis" if member states did not recover some of their lost policy autonomy.[10] Indeed, as his frustration grew, Prodi pronounced the Stability and Growth Pact to have been a "stupid" agreement.[11]

With the pact becoming an embarrassment for many national governments in the region and for the European Union itself, reforming the Stability and Growth Pact becomes an obvious policy option. There are several ways this could be done. One possibility would be to raise the budget deficit ceiling from 3 to 5 percent of GDP. Another possibility would be to make the fiscal limits adjustable to fit the differing conditions in EMU national economies. For example, the fiscal limit could be expanded in areas where economic growth has slowed, and then tightened as economic growth becomes stronger.

But reforming or even scrapping the Stability and Growth Pact might only delay a future EMU crisis. The very fact that there are different economic conditions among EMU member states reveals how Western Europe simply does not fit the basic criteria for an optimum currency area. Perhaps the European national economies were in the same phase of the business cycle during the late 1990s, thus making a common regional monetary policy appear appropriate given temporarily homogenous growth and inflation conditions on the Continent. But this economic homogeneity has effectively disappeared, if it ever really existed at all. Furthermore, Scheve's (2004) research has shown that even if national economic conditions were once relatively homogenous, national policy preferences, especially with regard to inflation, have never really been so.

This fact is critical because if the EMU project allows member governments to assert greater fiscal autonomy and if there are also varying preferences concerning government spending and its side effects (i.e., inflationary expectations), then fiscal policy divergence is certain to grow within the Eurozone. Furthermore, if there is greater fiscal policy divergence within the Eurozone, it will become even more difficult to find a common monetary policy appropri-

9. Thus far, Germany, France, Italy, and Portugal have clearly run up against the fiscal limits set by the Stability and Growth Pact (see *Economist* 2003c). In 2001, Ireland was also rebuked by the European Commission for its fiscal looseness (see *Economist* 2001a). In late 2004, Greece's budget was shown to have likely exceeded the limits set by the Stability and Growth Pact (see *Economist* 2004d). Together, these countries comprise more than 75 percent of the Eurozone's collective GDP.

10. Quoted in *Economist* 2002a.

11. Quoted in *Economist* 2002d.

ate for all participating national economies, putting the perfect exchange rate fixity offered by a common regional currency under increasing stress.

In fact, even with relatively limited fiscal policy divergence in Europe, the common regional monetary policy has already come under political stress. At first, it was criticized primarily by left-wing governments, who wanted a looser monetary policy to compensate for their apparent loss of fiscal policy autonomy through the Stability and Growth Pact.[12] But now the common European monetary policy has even drawn fire from right-wing governments, who prefer monetary expansion over fiscal expansion and see the European Central Bank's monetary stance as too tight given the recessionary economic environment in many parts of Europe.[13] To accommodate these governments, some observers have suggested that the European Central Bank raise its inflation target to something above 2 percent.[14] This would permit a lower nominal interest rate for the Eurozone, perhaps boosting private investment and helping to pacify increasingly dissatisfied right-wing governments. But this reform would remain a second-best economic expansion option for left-wing parties and their domestically oriented constituencies who demand the public goods afforded through greater government spending and that are likely to be undersupplied with only lower interest rates.

Another policy option that may become increasingly attractive, especially for leftist governments desiring greater policy autonomy to address domestic economic weaknesses, is to follow the example set by the British Labor Party and the Swedish Social Democrats, who elected to stay outside of the EMU. One might argue that exiting the EMU and giving up the common European currency entails high political and economic costs. This statement is certainly true, but it ignores the fact that remaining inside the EMU may eventually pose even greater opportunity costs for certain European governments. As the recent examples of Britain and Sweden further demonstrate, domestic policy autonomy is not at all inconsistent with strong macroeconomic performance. Since the final stage of the EMU was launched in 1999, GDP and employment growth in Britain and Sweden have been stronger than in most Eurozone national economies, with equally good, if not better, inflation outcomes.

If this gap continues or even widens, EMU exit may suddenly emerge as a very feasible policy option. Indeed, the failure to ratify the EU constitution in 2005 has allowed—even led—certain national policymakers in Europe to talk

12. See *Economist* 2001b.
13. See *Economist* 2004a.
14. See *Economist* 2002c, 2005a.

more openly about reintroducing the old national currencies.[15] If core EU states, such as Germany or France, exercise their exit option, then staying inside the Eurozone would become even less attractive for the remaining EMU member governments, with a potential ripple or cascade effect leading to the end of the supranational institution.

4. Extending the Research beyond the OECD

With the most recent expansion of the European Union, the new member states from Central and Eastern Europe are expected to move toward the EMU convergence criteria and eventually enter their national economies into the Eurozone, to the extent that this monetary arrangement remains functional.[16] This expectation raises a new research question not directly addressed in this book. Given international capital mobility, how do democratizing and non-democratic governments resolve the trade-off between domestic policy autonomy and exchange rate stability?

This book necessarily has focused its attention on the OECD governments, because, as discussed in chapter 1, these national economies—more developed and more democratic—represent the theoretical domain staked out by the systematic monetary convergence hypothesis. Less-democratic polities with less-developed economies had perhaps not yet entered the capitalist global economy and, thus, were not subject to the same pressures for external monetary convergence. But the OECD states are the core of the capitalist global economy and, as such, they should have been subject to all the pressures, both external and internal, for monetary policy convergence to achieve greater exchange rate stability. Since one of the primary objectives of this book was to examine this systematic monetary convergence proposition, it was necessary to test it on its most favorable theoretical domain. In focusing on the most developed and most democratic capitalist states in the international political economy, I have also left some theoretical and empirical space for scholars who may wish to explore similar research questions concerning nondemocratic and democratizing governments. For such scholars, I have provided some tractable operational measures that will assist in measuring domestic monetary autonomy and exchange rate stability for this larger set of states in the international system, although scholars should take care in assessing the validity of these measures,

15. See *Economist* 2005b.

16. On the difficulties facing these new EU member states as they adjust to the Eurozone, see Sadeh 2005.

given the more extensive capital controls that exist in many of these less-developed national economies.

In concluding this book, I will briefly speculate about how autocratic governments and democratizing states may resolve the trade-off between domestic policy autonomy and exchange rate stability as they fully enter the capitalist global economy. Although my conjectures build from the logic offered earlier in the book, I offer them only as very provisional hypotheses. Scholars may well prove them to be false.

I predict that nondemocratic governments will favor the choice for exchange rate stability and be more willing to accept the loss of domestic policy autonomy. This should be true for a couple of reasons. First, many autocratic states obtain political support from business interests in their national economy. Inasmuch as these favored business interests have cross-border commercial activities and, thus, expected preferences for exchange rate stability, they may be the only societal group able to transmit their economic policy preferences through the autocratic state bureaucracy. Second, since autocrats do not risk losing their political power in a popular election (although they do risk losing power in other ways and hence need political support from wealthy business interests), they should be more able than their democratic counterparts to ignore and even suppress the societal demands for domestic policy autonomy that inevitably emerge during periods of national economic weakness.

There is already some limited empirical support for this prediction. Although he offered a different logic to explain the result, Broz (2002, 873) demonstrated that states with a lower polity score (i.e., more autocratic) make exchange rate commitments that are more fixed in their character. While I have shown here that fixed exchange rate commitments are not good predictors of actual exchange rate stability for the developed economies (and this should be doubly true for developing ones), such political commitments may nonetheless indicate the autocracy's interest in external currency stability and its potential willingness to sacrifice domestic policy autonomy for this end.

I also predict that democratizing states may favor the choice for domestic policy autonomy. As societal groups obtain an increasingly important political role in setting national economic priorities and as they organize political parties to advance their economic policy preferences, it should become increasingly difficult for state leaders in transitional democracies to ignore societal demands for domestic policy autonomy and to maintain the commitments made by previous autocratic governments for fixed exchange rates. With reference to the interwar years, when many of the now-advanced industrial democracies were more akin to transitional democracies, Gilpin (1987, 129) observed how governments began to subordinate the external goal of exchange rate stability as they were forced to pay greater attention to "domestic welfare objectives such as [internal] economic stability and full employment."

Gilpin and other scholars have interpreted this interwar development, much like other such episodes of domestic policy autonomy, as a breakdown of international monetary cooperation. In many of these analyses, there appears to be a subtle normative argument that exchange rate stability is cooperative and good and that domestic policy autonomy is defective and bad. On this point, however, it may be very misleading to treat exchange rate stability as an unambiguous public good. Certainly, monetary policy choices have a distinct "public" character, but the choice for exchange rate stability is certainly not "good" for all citizens within democratic polities, both transitional and consolidated. Indeed, for the very large segment of the national political economy without strong cross-national business interests, exchange rate stability—with implications for both monetary and fiscal policy choices—may function largely as a "public bad." On this basis, the choice for domestic policy autonomy is not inconsistent with many important democratic ideals.

References

Achen, Christopher. 2000. Why Lagged Dependent Variables Can Suppress the Explanatory Power of Other Independent Variables. Paper presented at the annual meeting of the Society for Political Methodology, University of California, Los Angeles.

Alesina, Alberto, and Roberto Perotti. 1996. Income Distribution, Political Instability, and Investment. *European Economic Review* 40:1203–28.

Alesina, Alberto, and Howard Rosenthal. 1995. *Partisan Politics, Divided Government, and the Economy.* New York: Cambridge University Press.

Alesina, Alberto, and Lawrence H. Summers. 1993. Central Bank Independence and Macroeconomic Performance: Some Comparative Evidence. *Journal of Money, Credit, and Banking* 25 (May): 151–62.

Alt, James E. 1985. Political Parties, World Demand, and Unemployment: Domestic and International Sources of Economic Activity. *American Political Science Review* 79 (December): 1016–40.

Alt, James E., et al. 1996. The Political Economy of International Trade: Enduring Puzzles and an Agenda for Inquiry. *Comparative Political Studies* 29 (December): 689–717.

Andrews, David M. 1994a. Capital Mobility and Monetary Adjustment in Western Europe, 1973–1991. *Policy Sciences* 27:425–45.

Andrews, David M. 1994b. Capital Mobility and State Autonomy: Toward a Structural Theory of International Monetary Relations. *International Studies Quarterly* 38:193–218.

Aschauer, David Alan. 1990. *Public Investment and Private Sector Growth.* Washington, DC: Economic Policy Institute.

Axelrod, Robert, and Robert O. Keohane. 1986. Achieving Cooperation under Anarchy: Strategies and Institutions. In *Cooperation under Anarchy,* edited by Kenneth A. Oye, 226–54. Princeton: Princeton University Press.

Aylott, Nicholas. 2001. The Swedish Social Democracy Party. In *Social Democracy and Monetary Union,* edited by Ton Notermans, 149–74. New York: Berghahn Books.

Bacchetta, Philippe, and Eric van Wincoop. 2000. Does Exchange-Rate Stability Increase Trade and Welfare? *American Economic Review* 90 (December): 1093–1109.

Barnes, Ian. 1996. Monetary Integration and the 1995 Nordic Enlargement. In *The European Union and the Nordic Countries,* edited by Lee Miles, 169–85. New York: Routledge.

Barro, Robert. 1990. Government Spending in a Simple Model of Endogenous Growth. *Journal of Political Economy* 98 (October): 103–25.

Barro, Robert, and Xavier Sala-I-Martin. 1995. *Economic Growth.* New York: MacMillan.

Bearce, David H. 2002. Monetary Divergence: Domestic Political Institutions and the Policy Autonomy–Exchange Rate Stability Trade-off. *Comparative Political Studies* 35 (March): 194–220.

Bearce, David H. 2003. Societal Preferences, Partisan Agents, and Monetary Policy Outcomes. *International Organization* 57 (spring): 373–410.

Bearce, David H. 2005. Institutional Incompatibility: How Independent Central Banks Undermine Fixed Exchange Rate Commitments. Manuscript, University of Pittsburgh.

Beck, Nathaniel, and Jonathan N. Katz. 1995. What to Do (and Not to Do) with Time-Series Cross-Section Data. *American Political Science Review* 89 (September): 634–47.

Beck, Thorsten, et al. 2001. New Tools in Comparative Political Economy: The Database of Political Institutions. *World Bank Economic Review* 15 (September): 165–76.

Bell, D. S., and Byron Criddle. 1988. *The French Socialist Party: The Emergence of a Party of Government.* 2nd ed. Oxford: Clarendon.

Bernanke, Ben S., et al. 1999. *Inflation Targeting: Lessons from the International Experience.* Princeton: Princeton University Press.

Bernhard, William. 1998. A Political Explanation of Variations in Central Bank Independence. *American Political Science Review* 92 (June): 311–28.

Bernhard, William. 2002. *Banking on Reform: Political Parties and Central Bank Independence in the Industrial Democracies.* Ann Arbor: University of Michigan Press.

Bernhard, William, J. Lawrence Broz, and William Roberts Clark. 2002. The Political Economy of Monetary Institutions. *International Organization* 56 (autumn): 693–723.

Bernhard, William, and David Leblang. 1999. Democratic Institutions and Exchange Rate Commitments. *International Organization* 53 (winter): 71–97.

Bilger, Francois. 1993. The European Monetary System and French Monetary Policy. In *France and EC Membership Evaluated,* edited by Francois-George Dreyfus, Jacques Morizet, and Max Peyrard, 101–18. New York: St. Martin's.

Boix, Carles. 1997. Political Parties and the Supply Side of the Economy: The Provision of Physical and Human Capital in Advanced Economies, 1960–90. *American Journal of Political Science* 41 (July): 814–45.

Boix, Carles. 1998. *Political Parties, Growth, and Equality: Conservative and Social Democratic Economic Strategies in the World Economy.* New York: Cambridge University Press.

Broz, J. Lawrence. 2002. Political System Transparency and Monetary Commitment Regimes. *International Organization* 56 (autumn): 861–87.

Broz, J. Lawrence, and Jeffry A. Frieden. 2001. The Political Economy of International Monetary Relations. *Annual Review of Political Science* 4:317–43.

Bryant, Ralph. 1987. *International Financial Regulation.* Washington, DC: Brookings Institution.

Burgoon, Brian. 2001. Globalization and Welfare Compensation: Disentangling the Ties That Bind. *International Organization* 55 (summer): 509–51.

Buti, Marco, Werner Roeger, and Jan In't Veld. 2001. Monetary and Fiscal Policy Interactions under a Stability Pact. European University Institute Working Papers no. 2001/8.

Calvo, Guillermo, and Carmen M. Reinhart. 2002. Fear of Floating. *Quarterly Journal of Economics* 117 (May): 379–408.

Cargill, Thomas F., Michael M. Hutchison, and Takatoshi Ito. 1997. *The Political Economy of Japanese Monetary Policy.* Cambridge, MA: MIT Press.

Cerny, Phil. 1993. The Deregulation and Re-regulation of Financial Markets in a More Open World. In *Finance and World Politics,* edited by Phil Cerny, 51–85. Aldershot, UK: Edward Elgar.

Cerny, Phil. 1995. Globalization and the Changing Logic of Collective Action. *International Organization* 49 (autumn): 595–625.

Clark, William Roberts. 2002. Partisan and Electoral Motivations and the Choice of Monetary Institutions under Fully Mobile Capital. *International Organization* 56 (autumn): 725–49.

Clark, William Roberts. 2003. *Capitalism, Not Globalism: Capital Mobility, Central Bank Independence, and the Political Control of the Economy.* Ann Arbor: University of Michigan Press.

Clark, William Roberts, and Mark Hallerberg. 2000. Mobile Capital, Domestic Institutions, and Electorally Induced Monetary and Fiscal Policy. *American Political Science Review* 94 (June): 323–46.

Clark, William Roberts, and Usha Nair Reichert. 1998. International and Domestic Constraints on Political Business Cycles in OECD Economies. *International Organization* 52 (winter): 87–120.

Cobham, David. 2002. *The Making of Monetary Policy in the UK, 1975–2000: Series of Financial Economics and Quantitative Analysis.* Hoboken, NJ: John Wiley and Sons.

Cohen, Benjamin J. 1993. The Triad and the Unholy Trinity: Lessons for the Pacific Region. In *Pacific Economic Relations in the 1990s: Cooperation or Conflict?* edited by Richard Higgott et al., 133–58. Boulder, CO: Lynne Rienner.

Cohen, Benjamin J. 1995. A Brief History of International Monetary Relations. In *International Political Economy,* edited by Jeffry A. Frieden and David A. Lake, 209–29. 3rd ed. New York: St. Martin's.

Cohen, Benjamin J. 1996. Phoenix Risen: The Resurrection of Global Finance. *World Politics* 48 (January): 268–96.

Cole, Alistair. 1994. A House Divided: Socialism à la française. In *France during the Socialist Years,* edited by Gino Raymond, 64–89. Brookfield, VT: Dartmouth Publishing.

Commission of the European Communities. 1990. One Market, One Money. *European Economy* 44 (October).

Cooper, Richard N. 1994. International Policy Coordination. *Journal of International Affairs* 48 (summer): 287–93.

Crystal, Jonathan. 2004. Globalization and Economic Policy: What Has Changed? *International Studies Review* 6, no. 3 (September): 467–69.

Cukierman, Alex, Steven B. Webb, and Bilin Neyapti. 1992. Measuring the Independence of Central Banks and Its Effect on Policy Outcomes. *World Bank Economic Review* 6 (September): 353–98.

Cusack, Thomas R. 1999. Partisan Politics and Fiscal Policy. *Comparative Political Studies* 32 (June): 464–86.

De Gregorio, Jose, Alberto Giovannini, and Holger C. Wolf. 1994. International Evidence on Tradables and Nontradables Inflation. *European Economic Review* 38:1225–44.

Denver, David. 1998. The British Electorate in the 1990s. In *Britain in the Nineties: The Politics of Paradox,* edited by Hugh Berrington, 197–217. Portland, OR: Frank Cass.

Downs, Anthony. 1957. *An Economic Theory of Democracy.* New York: Harper.

Drezner, Daniel W. 2001. Globalization and Policy Convergence. *International Studies Review* 3 (spring): 53–78.

Eckstein, Harry. 1975. Case Study and Theory in Political Science. In *Handbook of Political Science,* vol. 1, *Political Science: Scope and Theory,* edited by Fred I. Greenstein and Nelson W. Polsby, 79–133. Reading, MA: Addison-Wesley.

Eckstein, Otto. 1980. *Core Inflation.* Englewood Cliffs, NJ: Prentice-Hall.

Economist. 2001a. Ireland's Euro-sins. February 17, 24.

Economist. 2001b. European Economies: France 1, Germany 0. March 17, 74–75.

Economist. 2001c. The Second Term: Tony's Big Ambitions. June 9, 59.

Economist. 2002a. Europe's Big Idea. January 5, 11.

Economist. 2002b. Britain and the Euro: Fit to Join? February 9, 48.

Economist. 2002c. Re-engineering the Euro. October 19, 72.

Economist. 2002d. Restoring Europe's Smile. October 26, 11.

Economist. 2003a. Britain and the Euro: Five Tests and a Funeral. May 3, 57.

Economist. 2003b. Waiting for Blair. May 3, 56.

Economist. 2003c. Loosening Those Bonds. July 19, 38–39.

Economist. 2004a. Back to the 1970s? June 19, 11.

Economist. 2004b. Global Inflation: A Ghost from the Past. June 19, 69–70.

Economist. 2004c. Inflated Expectations. July 3, 64.

Economist. 2004d. Greece and the Euro: Reality Check. October 2, 51.

Economist. 2005a. And Now, the Euro. June 11, 11.

Economist. 2005b. The Euro and Its Troubles. June 11, 69–70.

Edison, Hali J., and Michael Melvin. 1990. The Determinants and Implications of the Choice of an Exchange Rate System. In *Monetary Policy for a Volatile Global Economy,* edited by William S. Haraf and Thomas D. Willett, 1–44. Washington, DC: AEI Press.

Eichengreen, Barry. 1992. Should the Maastricht Treaty Be Saved? Princeton Studies in International Finance 74. Princeton, NJ: International Finance Section, Department of Economics, Princeton University.

Eichengreen, Barry. 1996. *Globalizing Capital: A History of the International Monetary System.* Princeton: Princeton University Press.

Elgie, Robert, and Helen Thompson. 1998. *The Politics of Central Banks.* New York: Routledge.

Esping-Andersen, Gosta. 1999. Politics without Class: Postindustrial Cleavages in Europe and America. In *Continuity and Change in Contemporary Capitalism,* edited by Herbert Kitschelt et al., 293–316. New York: Cambridge University Press.

Evans, Geoffrey. 1999. *The End of Class Politics? Class Voting in Comparative Context.* Oxford: Oxford University Press.

Fama, E. F. 1984. Forward and Spot Exchange Rates. *Journal of Monetary Economics* 14 (November): 319–38.

Favero, Carlo. 2002. How Do European Monetary and Fiscal Authorities Behave? IGIER Working Paper 214, Innocenzo Gasparini Institute for Economic Research, Milan.

Ferguson, Thomas, and Joel Rogers. 1986. *Right Turn: The Decline of the Democrats and the Future of American Politics.* New York: Hill and Wang.

Fielding, Steven. 1999. *Labour Decline and Renewal.* 2nd ed. Wiltshire, UK: Baseline.

Fleming, Marcus. 1962. Domestic Financial Policies under Fixed and under Floating Exchange Rates. *IMF Staff Papers* 9:369–80.

Fordham, Benjamin O., and Timothy J. McKeown. 2003. Selection and Influence: Interest Groups and Congressional Voting on Trade Policy. *International Organization* 57 (summer): 519–49.

Frankel, Jeffrey A. 1991. Quantifying International Capital Mobility in the 1980s. In *National Saving and Economic Performance,* edited by Douglas Bernheim and John Shover, 227–70. Chicago: University of Chicago Press.

Frankel, Jeffrey A., and K. A. Froot. 1989. Forward Discount Bias: Is It an Exchange Rate Risk Premium? *Quarterly Journal of Economics* 104 (February): 139–61.

Frankel, Jeffrey A., Sergio L. Schmukler, and Luis Serven. 2002. Global Transmission of Interest Rates: Monetary Independence and Currency Regime. NBER Working Paper 8828, National Bureau of Economic Research, Cambridge, MA.

Fratianni, Michele, and Franco Spinelli. 1997. *A Monetary History of Italy.* New York: Cambridge University Press.

Fratianni, Michele, and Jurgen von Hagen. 1992. *The European Monetary System and European Monetary Union.* Boulder, CO: Westview.

Freeman, John R., Jude C. Hayes, and Helmut Stix. 2000. Democracy and Markets: The Case of Exchange Rates. *American Journal of Political Science* 44 (July): 449–68.

Frieden, Jeffry A. 1991. Invested Interests: The Politics of National Economic Policies in a World of Global Finance. *International Organization* 45 (autumn): 425–51.

Frieden, Jeffry A. 2002. Real Sources of European Currency Policy: Sectoral Interests and European Monetary Integration. *International Organization* 56 (autumn): 831–60.

Friedman, Milton. 1953. The Case for Flexible Exchange Rates. In *Essays in Positive Economics,* edited by Milton Friedman, 157–203. Chicago: University of Chicago Press.

Friedman, Milton. 1968. The Role of Monetary Policy. *American Economic Review* 58 (March): 1–17.

Friedman, Thomas L. 1999. *The Lexus and the Olive Tree.* New York: Farrar, Straus, and Giroux.

Froot, Kenneth A., and Kenneth Rogoff. 1991. The EMS, the EMU, and the Transition to a Common Currency. In *NBER Macroeconomics Annual 1991,* edited by Olivier Jean Blanchard and Stanley Fisher, 269–317. Cambridge, MA: MIT Press.

Funabashi, Yoichi. 1988. *Managing the Dollar: From the Plaza to the Louvre.* Washington, DC: Institute for International Economics.

Gamble, Andrew. 1994. *The Free Economy and the Strong State: The Politics of Thatcherism.* 2nd ed. London: Macmillan.

Gamble, Andrew, and Gavin Kelly. 2002. Britain and EMU. In *European States and the Euro,* edited by Kenneth Dyson, 97–119. New York: Oxford University Press.

Garrett, Geoffrey. 1995. Capital Mobility, Trade, and the Domestic Politics of Economic Policy. *International Organization* 49 (autumn): 657–87.

Garrett, Geoffrey. 1998a. Global Markets and National Politics: Collision Course or Virtuous Circle? *International Organization* 52 (autumn): 787–824.

Garrett, Geoffrey. 1998b. *Partisan Politics in the Global Economy.* New York: Cambridge University Press.

Garrett, Geoffrey. 2000. Capital Mobility, Exchange Rates, and Fiscal Policy in the Global Economy. *Review of International Political Economy* 7 (spring): 153–70.

Garrett, Geoffrey, and Peter Lange. 1991. Political Responses to Interdependence: What's "Left" for the Left? *International Organization* 45 (autumn): 539–64.

Garrett, Geoffrey, and Peter Lange. 1995. Internationalization, Institutions, and Political Change. *International Organization* 49 (autumn): 627–55.

Gilpin, Robert. 1987. *The Political Economy of International Relations.* Princeton: Princeton University Press.

Gilpin, Robert. 2001. *Global Political Economy: Understanding the International Economic Order.* Princeton: Princeton University Press.

Gobbin, Niko, and Bas Van Aarle. 2001. Fiscal Adjustments and Their Effects during the Transition to the EMU. *Public Choice* 109:269–99.

Gold, Joseph. 1977. International Capital Movements under the Law of the International Monetary Fund. IMF Pamphlet Series 21. Washington, DC: International Monetary Fund.

Goodman, John B. 1992. *Monetary Sovereignty: The Politics of Central Banking in Western Europe.* Ithaca: Cornell University Press.

Goodman, John B., and Louis W. Pauly. 1993. The Obsolescence of Capital Controls? Economic Management in an Age of Global Markets. *World Politics* 46 (October): 50–82.

Gowa, Joanne. 1983. *Closing the Gold Window: Domestic Politics and the End of the Bretton Woods.* Ithaca: Cornell University Press.

Gowa, Joanne. 1988. Public Goods and Political Institutions: Trade and Monetary Policy Processes in the United States. *International Organization* 42 (winter): 15–32.

Greider, William. 1997. *One World, Ready or Not: The Manic Logic of Global Capitalism.* New York: Simon and Schuster.

Grilli, Vittorio, Donato Masciandaro, and Guido Tabellini. 1991. Political and Monetary Institutions and Public Financial Policies in the Industrial Countries. *Economic Policy* 13 (October): 342–92.

Grilli, Vittorio, and Gian Maria Milesi-Ferretti. 1995. Economic Effects and Structural Determinants of Capital Controls. *IMF Staff Papers* 42:517–51.

Gros, Daniel, and Niels Thygesen. 1992. *European Monetary Integration.* London: Longman.

Grubaugh, Stephen, and Scott Sumner. 1990. Monetary Policy and the U.S. Trade Deficit. In *The Reagan Years: The Record in Presidential Leadership,* edited by Joseph Hogan, 237–58. New York: Manchester University Press.

Hall, Peter A. 1986. *Governing the Economy: The Politics of State Intervention in Britain and France.* New York: Oxford University Press.

Hall, Peter A., and David Soskice. 2001. *Varieties of Capitalism: The Institutional Foundations of Comparative Advantage.* New York: Oxford University Press.

Hallerberg, Mark. 2002. Veto Players and the Choice of Monetary Institutions. *International Organization* 56 (autumn): 775–802.

Hayward, Jack. 1986. *The State and the Market Economy: Industrial Patriotism and Economic Intervention in France.* Sussex, UK: Wheatsheaf Books.

Healy, Conor. 2004. Sustaining an Exchange Rate Fix: An Integrated Approach to Understanding Survival. Paper presented at the American Political Science Association annual meeting, Chicago.

Helleiner, Eric. 1994. *States and the Reemergence of Global Finance: From Bretton Woods to the 1990s.* Ithaca: Cornell University Press.

Henning, C. Randall. 1994. *Currencies and Politics in the United States, Germany, and Japan.* Washington, DC: Institute for International Economics.

Hibbs, Douglas A. 1977. Political Parties and Macroeconomic Policy. *American Political Science Review* 71:1467–87.

Himmelstein, Jerome L. 1990. *To the Right: The Transformation of American Conservatism.* Berkeley: University of California Press.

Hout, Michael, Jeff Manza, and Clem Brooks. 1999. Classes, Unions, and the Realignment of U.S. Presidential Voting, 1952–1992. In *The End of Class Politics? Class Voting in Comparative Context,* edited by Geoffrey Evans, 83–96. New York: Oxford University Press.

Howarth, David J. 2001. *The French Road to European Monetary Union.* New York: Palgrave.

Howarth, David J. 2002. EMU, Integration Theories, and the Annoying Complexities of French Policy-Making. In *The Euro: European Integration Theory and Economic and Monetary Union,* edited by Amy Verdun, 179–99. Lanham, MD: Rowman and Littlefield.

Iida, Keisuke. 1993. Analytic Uncertainty and International Cooperation: Theory and Application to International Economic Policy Coordination. *International Studies Quarterly* 37:431–57.

International Monetary Fund. 1973–93. *International Financial Statistics.* CD-ROM.

Iversen, Torben, and Thomas R. Cusack. 2000. The Causes of Welfare State Expansion: Deindustrialization or Globalization? *World Politics* 52 (April): 313–49.

Iversen, Torben, and Anne Wren. 1998. Equality, Employment, and Budgetary Restraint: The Trilemma of the Service Economy. *World Politics* 50 (July): 507–46.

Jacobs, David C. D. 1999. *Business Lobbies and the Power Structure in America: Evidence and Arguments.* Westport, CT: Quorum Books.

Jankowski, Richard, and Christopher Wleizen. 1993. Substitutability and the Politics of Macroeconomic Policy. *Journal of Politics* 55 (November): 1060–80.

Johnson, Peter A. 1998. *The Government of Money: Monetarism in Germany and the United States.* Ithaca: Cornell University Press.

Karier, Thomas. 1997. *Great Experiments in American Economic Policy: From Kennedy to Reagan.* Westport, CT: Praeger.

Keele, Luke, and Nathan J. Kelly. 2004. Dynamic Models for Dynamic Theories: The Ins and Outs of Lagged Dependent Variables. Manuscript, Oxford University and University of North Carolina.

Keohane, Robert O. 1984. *After Hegemony: Cooperation and Discord in the World Political Economy.* Princeton: Princeton University Press.

Kettl, Donald F. 1986. *Leadership at the Fed.* New Haven: Yale University Press.

Kirschen, E. S., et al. 1964. *Economic Policy in Our Time.* Vol. 1. Amsterdam: North-Holland.

Kitschelt, Herbert, et al. 1999. *Continuity and Change in Contemporary Capitalism.* New York: Cambridge University Press.

Kristensen, Ida P., and Gregory Wawro. 2003. Lagging the Dog? The Robustness of Panel Corrected Standard Errors in the Presence of Serial Correlation and Observation Specific Effects. Paper presented at the annual meeting of the Society for Political Methodology, University of Minneapolis.

Krugman, Paul. 1999. The Return of Depression Economics. *Foreign Affairs,* January–February, 56–74.

Kurzer, Paulette. 1993. *Business and Banking: Political Change and Economic Integration in Western Europe.* Ithaca: Cornell University Press.

Lane, Jan-Erik, David McKay, and Kenneth Newton. 1997. *Political Data Handbook: OECD Countries.* Oxford: Oxford University Press.

Lawson, Nigel. 1992. *The View from No. 11: Memoirs of a Tory Radical.* London: Bantam.

Leertouwer, Erik, and Philipp Maier. 2002. International and Domestic Constraints on Political Business Cycles in OECD Economies: A Comment. *International Organization* (winter): 209–21.

Levine, Ross, and David Renelt. 1992. A Sensitivity Analysis of Cross-Country Growth Regressions. *American Economic Review* 82 (September): 942–63.

Levy-Yeyati, Eduardo, and Federico Sturzenegger. 2003. To Float or to Fix: Evidence on the Impact of Exchange Rate Regimes on Growth. *American Economic Review* 93 (September): 1173–93.

Levy-Yeyati, Eduardo, and Federico Sturzenegger. 2005. Classifying Exchange Rate Regimes: Deeds vs. Words. *European Economic Review* 49:1603–35.

Loriaux, Michael. 1991. *France after Hegemony: International Change and Financial Reform.* Ithaca: Cornell University Press.

Manheim, Jarol B., Richard C. Rich, and Lars Willnat. 2002. *Empirical Political Analysis: Research Methods of Political Science.* 5th ed. New York: Longman.

Marston, Richard C. 1995. *International Financial Integration: A Study of Interest Differentials between the Major Industrial Countries.* New York: Cambridge University Press.

McNamara, Kathleen R. 1998. *The Currency of Ideas: Monetary Politics in the European Union.* Ithaca: Cornell University Press.

Melitz, Jacques. 1997. Some Cross-Country Evidence about Debt, Deficits, and the Behavior of Monetary and Fiscal Authorities. CEPR Discussion Paper 1653. Centre for Economic Policy Research, London.

Melitz, Jacques. 2000. Some Cross-Country Evidence about Fiscal Policy Behavior and Consequences for EMU. Manuscript, University of Strathclyde, UK.

Milner, Helen V., and Robert O. Keohane. 1996. Internationalization and Domestic Politics: A Conclusion. In *Internationalization and Domestic Politics,* edited by Robert O. Keohane and Helen V. Milner, 243–58. New York: Cambridge University Press.

Minford, Patrick. 1993. The United Kingdom. In *Monetary Policy in Developed Economies,* edited by Michele U. Fratianni and Dominick Salvatore, 405–31. Westport, CT: Greenwood.

Moses, Jonathon W. 1994. Abdication from National Policy Autonomy: What's Left to Leave. *Politics and Society* 22 (June): 125–48.

Moses, Jonathon W. 1998. Sweden and EMU. In *Joining Europe's Monetary Club: The Challenges for Smaller Member States,* edited by Erik Jones et al., 203–24. New York: St. Martin's.

Mosley, Layna. 2000. Room to Move: International Financial Markets and National Welfare States. *International Organization* 54 (autumn): 737–73.

Muet, Pierre-Alain, and Alain Fonteneau. 1990. *Reflation and Austerity: Economic Policy under Mitterrand.* New York: Berg.

Mundell, Robert A. 1960. The Monetary Dynamics of International Adjustment under Fixed and Flexible Exchange Rates. *Quarterly Journal of Economics* 74 (May): 227–50.

Mundell, Robert A. 1963. Capital Mobility and Stabilization Policy under Fixed and Flexible Exchange Rates. *Canadian Journal of Economics and Political Science* 29 (November): 475–85.

Mundell, Robert A. 1968. *International Economics.* New York: Macmillan.

Notermans, Ton. 1993. The Abdication from National Policy Autonomy: Why the Macroeconomic Policy Regime Has Become so Unfavorable to Labor. *Politics and Society* 21 (June): 133–67.

Nurkse, Ragnar. 1944. *International Currency Experience: Lessons from the Interwar Period.* Geneva: League of Nations.

Oatley, Thomas. 1997. *Monetary Politics: Exchange Rate Cooperation in the European Union.* Ann Arbor: University of Michigan Press.

Oatley, Thomas. 1999. How Constraining Is Capital Mobility? The Partisan Hypothesis in an Open Economy. *American Journal of Political Science* 43 (October): 1003–27.

Obstfeld, Maurice, and Kenneth Rogoff. 1995. The Mirage of Fixed Exchange Rates. *Journal of Economic Perspectives* 9 (fall): 73–96.

Ohmae, Kenichi. 1995. *The End of the Nation State: The Rise of Regional Economies.* New York: Free Press.

Organization for Economic Cooperation and Development. *Annual National Accounts.* CD-ROM.

Oye, Kenneth A. 1986. Explaining Cooperation under Anarchy: Hypotheses and Strategies. In *Cooperation under Anarchy,* edited by Kenneth A. Oye, 1–24. Princeton: Princeton University Press.

Pauly, Louis W. 1995. Capital Mobility, State Autonomy, and Political Legitimacy. *Journal of International Affairs* 48 (winter): 369–88.

Phelps, Edmund. 1968. Money Wage Dynamics and Labor Market Equilibrium. *Journal of Political Economy* 76, no. 4, pt. 2: 678–711.

Philip, Alan Butt. 1992. British Pressure Groups and the European Community. In *Britain and the European Community: The Politics of Semi-Detachment,* edited by Stephen George, 149–71. Oxford: Clarendon.

Phillips, A. W. 1958. The Relationship between Unemployment and the Rate of Change of Money Wages in the United Kingdom, 1861–1957. *Economica* 25 (November): 283–99.

Pilkington, Colin. 2001. *Britain in the European Union Today.* 2nd ed. Manchester, UK: Manchester University Press.

Posner, Alan R. 1978. Italy: Dependence and Political Fragmentation. In *Between Power and Plenty: Foreign Economic Policies of Advanced Industrial States,* edited by Peter J. Katzenstein, 225–54. Madison: University of Wisconsin Press.

Putnam, Robert D. 1988. Diplomacy and Domestic Politics: The Logic of Two-Level Games. *International Organization* 42 (summer): 427–60.

Putnam, Robert D., and Nicholas Bayne. 1987. *Hanging Together: Cooperation and Conflict in the Seven-Power Summits.* Cambridge, MA: Harvard University Press.

Putnam, Robert D., and C. Randall Henning. 1989. The Bonn Summit of 1978: A Case Study in Coordination. In *Can Nations Agree? Issues in International Economic Cooperation,* edited by Richard N. Cooper et al., 12–140. Washington, DC: Brookings Institution.

Quinn, Dennis, and Carla Inclan. 1997. The Origins of Financial Openness: A Study of Current and Capital Account Liberalization. *American Journal of Political Science* 41 (July): 771–813.

Quinn, Dennis P., and Robert Y. Shapiro. 1991. Economic Growth Strategies: The Effects of Ideological Partisanship on Interest Rates and Business Taxation in the United States. *American Journal of Political Science* 35 (August): 656–85.

Reinhart, Carmen M., and Kenneth S. Rogoff. 2004. The Modern History of Exchange Rate Arrangements: A Reinterpretation. *Quarterly Journal of Economics* 119 (February): 1–48.

Ringe, Nils F. 2003. Budgetary Constraint or Device for Collective Fiscal Retrenchment? The Maastricht Convergence Criteria and Social Spending in the EU Member States. Manuscript, University of Pittsburgh.

Romer, Paul M. 1990. Endogenous Technological Change. *Journal of Political Economy* 98 (October): 79–102.

Rose, Andrew K. 1994. Exchange Rate Volatility, Monetary Policy, and Capital Mobility: Empirical Evidence on the Holy Trinity. NBER Working Paper 4630, National Bureau of Economic Research, Cambridge, MA.

Ross, George. 2001. French Social Democracy and EMU: Presidential Prose and Its Pitfalls. In *Social Democracy and Monetary Union,* edited by Ton Notermans, 21–46. New York: Berghahn Books.

Roubini, Nouriel, and Jeffrey Sachs. 1989. Government Spending and Budget Deficits in the Industrial Countries. *Economic Policy* 8 (April): 99–132.

Rowen, Hobart. Blumenthal: Dollar's Fall Nearly Over. *Washington Post,* July 22, D6.

Rudra, Nita. 2002. Globalization and the Decline of the Welfare State in Less-Developed Countries. *International Organization* 56 (spring): 411–45.

Ruggie, John Gerard. 1982. International Regimes, Transactions, and Change: Embedded Liberalism in the Postwar Economic Order. *International Organization* 36 (spring): 379–415.

Ryan, Mike H., Carl L. Swanson, and Rogene A. Buchholz. 1987. *Corporate Strategy, Public Policy, and the Fortune 500: How America's Major Corporations Influence Government.* New York: Basil Blackwell.

Sadeh, Tal. 2005. Who Can Adjust to the Euro? *World Economy* 28 (11): 1651–78.

Scharpf, Fritz. 1991. *Crisis and Choice in European Social Democracy.* Ithaca: Cornell University Press.

Scheve, Kenneth. 2004. Public Inflation Aversion and the Political Economy of Macroeconomic Policymaking. *International Organization* 58 (winter): 1–34.

Schrodt, Philip A. 2004. Review of *The Behavioral Origins of War,* by D. Scott Bennett and Allan C. Stam. *Perspectives on Politics* 2 (December): 886–87.

Schulze, Gunther G., and Heinrich W. Ursprung. 1999. Globalisation of the Economy and the Nation State. *World Economy* 22 (3): 295–352.

Seldon, Anthony, and Daniel Collins. 2000. *Britain under Thatcher: Seminar Studies in History.* New York: Longman.

Shambaugh, Jay C. 2004. The Effect of Fixed Exchange Rates on Monetary Policy. *Quarterly Journal of Economics* 119 (February): 301–52.

Shepherd, William F. 1994. *International Financial Integration: History, Theory, and Application in OECD Countries.* Burlington, VT: Ashgate.

Silk Leonard, and David Vogel. 1977. *Profits and Principles: The Social and Political Thinking of American Businessmen.* New York: Simon and Schuster.

Simmons, Beth A. 1996. Rulers of the Game: Central Bank Independence during the Interwar Years. *International Organization* 50 (summer): 407–43.

Simmons, Beth A. 1999. The Internationalization of Capital. In *Continuity and Change in Contemporary Capitalism,* edited by Herbert Kitschelt et al., 36–69. New York: Cambridge University Press.

Smyser, W. R. 1993. Goodbye, G-7. *Washington Quarterly* 16 (winter): 15–28.

Sterling-Folker, Jennifer. 2002. *Theories of International Cooperation and the Primacy of Anarchy: Explaining U.S. International Monetary Policy-Making after Bretton Woods.* Albany: State University of New York Press.

Stockman, David A. 1986. *The Triumph of Politics: How the Reagan Revolution Failed.* New York: Harper and Row.

Stone, Charles F., and Isabel V. Sawhill. 1984. *Economic Policy in the Reagan Years.* Washington, DC: Urban Institute Press.

Suzuki, Takaaki. 2000. *Japan's Budget Politics: Balancing Domestic and International Interests.* Boulder, CO: Lynne Rienner.

Takenaka, Heizo. 1991. *Contemporary Japanese Economy and Economic Policy.* Ann Arbor: University of Michigan Press.

Talani, Leila Simona. 2000. *Betting for and against EMU: Who Wins and Who Loses in Italy and in the UK from the Process of European Monetary Integration.* Brookfield, VT: Ashgate.

Temperton, Paul. 1991. *UK Monetary Policy: The Challenge for the 1990s.* London: Macmillan.

Thompson, Helen. 1996. *The British Conservative Government and the European Exchange Rate Mechanism, 1979–1994.* London: Pinter.

Thygesen, Niels. 1982. Monetary Policy. In *The European Economy: Growth and Crisis,* edited by Andrea Boltho, 329–64. New York: Oxford University Press.

Tinbergen, Jan. 1966. *On the Theory of Economic Policy.* Amsterdam: North-Holland.

Ungerer, Horst. 1997. *A Concise History of European Monetary Integration: From EPU to EMU.* Westport, CT: Quorum Books.

Vaubel, Roland. 1989. A Critical Assessment of EMS. Paper presented at the Financial Times Conferences on World Banking, November 30–December 1, 1989, London, UK.

Verdier, Daniel. 1998. Domestic Responses to Capital Market Internationalization under the Gold Standard, 1870–1914. *International Organization* 52 (winter): 1–34.

Von Hagen, Jurgen, and Rolf R. Strauch. 2001. Fiscal Consolidations: Quality, Economic Conditions, and Success. *Public Choice* 109:327–46.

Walsh, James I. 2000. When Do Ideas Matter? Explaining the Successes and Failures of Thatcherite Ideas. *Comparative Political Studies* 33 (May): 483–516.

Waltz, Kenneth N. 1979. *Theory of International Politics.* New York: McGraw-Hill.

Watson, Alison M. S. 1997. *Aspects of European Monetary Integration: The Politics of Convergence.* New York: St. Martin's.

Way, Christopher. 2000. Central Banks, Partisan Politics, and Macroeconomic Outcomes. *Comparative Political Studies* 33 (March): 196–224.

Weatherford, M. Stephen, and Lorraine M. McDonnell. 1990. Ideology and Economic Policy. In *Looking Back on the Reagan Presidency,* edited by Larry Berman, 122–55. Baltimore: Johns Hopkins University Press.

Webb, Michael C. 1991. International Economic Structures, Government Interests, and International Coordination of Macroeconomic Adjustment Policies. *International Organization* 45 (summer): 309–42.

Webb, Michael C. 1994. Capital Mobility and the Possibilities for International Policy Coordination. *Policy Sciences* 27:395–423.

Webb, Michael C. 1995. *The Political Economy of Policy Coordination: International Adjustment since 1945.* Ithaca: Cornell University Press.

Willett, Thomas D., Wassem Khan, and Aida Der Hovanessian. 1985. Interest Rate Changes, Inflationary Expectations, and Exchange Rate Overshooting: The Dollar-

DM Rate. In *Exchange Rates, Trade, and the U.S. Economy,* edited by Sven W. Arndt et al., 49–71. Cambridge, MA: Ballinger.

Woldendorp, Jaap, Hans Keman, and Ian Budge. 1993. Political Data, 1945–1990: Party Governments in 20 Democracies. *European Journal of Political Research* 24:1–120.

Woolley, John. 1992. Policy Credibility and European Monetary Institutions. In *Euro-Politics: Institutions and Policymaking in the New European Community,* edited by Alberta Sbragia, 157–90. Washington, DC: Brookings Institution.

World Bank. *World Development Indicators.* CD-ROM.

Index

Note: Italicized page numbers indicate figure or table.

153